T0146709

When Forgiveness Doesn't Make Sense

When Forgiveness Doesn't Make Sense

Robert Jeffress

WaterBrook
Press

WHEN FORGIVENESS DOESN'T MAKE SENSE

Some of the stories in this book are composites of several different situations; details and names have been changed to protect identities.

Trade Paperback ISBN 978-1-57856-464-4
eBook ISBN 978-0-307-83068-5

Published in association with Sealy M. Yates, Literary Agent, Orange, California.

Published in the United States by WaterBrook, an imprint of the Crown Publishing Group, a division of Penguin Random House LLC, New York.

Library of Congress Cataloging-in-Publication Data
Jeffress, Robert, 1955–
When forgiveness doesn't make sense / Robert Jeffress — 1st ed.
p. cm.
ISBN 1-57856-464-6 (pbk.)
1. Forgiveness—Religious aspects—Christianity. I. Title.
BV4647.F55J44 2000
234'.5—dc21
99-059441

147429898

FOR MY UNCLE, JIM FIELDER,

who continues to be a source of strength and encouragement for our family

CONTENTS

Acknowledgments

No book (at least one worth reading) is a solo effort. I am indebted to a number of people for their partnership in this effort, including…

Dan Rich, Steve Cobb, and the team at WaterBrook Press for your enthusiasm for this project from the beginning.

Thomas Womack for your assistance in skillfully crafting this manuscript into its final form.

The many other authors who have provided grist for this writer's mill. I am particularly grateful for the writings of Lewis Smedes, whom I quote throughout the book. While I have attempted to footnote every idea and quote that was not my own, I am sure I have failed. If any author has been slighted, please forgive me.

My friends and agents Sealy Yates and Tom Thompson for their encouragement through the years.

The members of First Baptist Church, Wichita Falls, Texas, for your enthusiastic response to the ideas presented in this book and your love for your pastor.

And most of all, my family — Amy, Julia, and Dorothy — for constantly extending forgiveness to a flawed husband and imperfect dad, who loves you dearly.

Part One

Understanding Forgiveness

CHAPTER 1

THE VIEW FROM THE PULPIT

Why the forgiven are not always the best forgivers

When Jerry Fuller came to see me, he felt like the world's biggest fool. Everyone on the planet it seemed — everyone except Jerry — had known that his wife, Misty, was sleeping with his best friend, Phil.

Phil and Jerry had been college roommates and later had started a software consulting firm together. They each married within a few months of one another, and during those first years Jerry and Misty spent several nights a week with Phil and Heather doing everything from addressing advertising flyers to catching a cheap movie at the local dollar theater. Jerry wasn't alarmed to see Misty laughing at Phil's jokes more than his own. In fact, he was grateful that his wife and his best friend appeared to enjoy each other so much.

Now, years later, the couples still got together frequently. But one night something happened that awakened Jerry's suspicions. As they made their way to their seats at a Christian concert, he noticed how

Misty made a point of making sure she was seated next to Phil. Throughout the concert she and Phil kept whispering and snickering.

"What was the deal with you and Phil tonight?" Jerry inquired on the ride home, not even trying to hide the edge in his voice.

"Nothing," Misty answered matter-of-factly. "We've always thought the same things were funny, that's all."

Over the next several weeks, Jerry became more aware of irregularities that might otherwise have gone unnoticed. Sometimes when he would return home early, Misty would abruptly end the phone conversation with "Sorry, Jerry's home, gotta go." Increasingly, when Jerry answered the phone, the other party would quickly hang up. And then there were Misty's unexplained absences in the evening. Sometimes the phone would ring and Misty would race to answer it. After only a few seconds of conversation, Misty would suddenly remember "something I need at the store" and be gone for several hours.

It was one of those evenings that finally brought everything to a head. After a brief call, answered before a first full ring, Misty announced, "I'm running over to Heather's to give her some ideas on her redecorating project." When the minutes turned into several hours, Jerry called to check on Misty.

"No, she hasn't been here all evening," Heather responded.

On a hunch, Jerry asked, "Can I speak to Phil for a moment?"

"You're out of luck tonight. Phil's not here either. He's at the office working late on the Laraby project."

After another hour Misty finally arrived home, mumbled a brief hello, and hurried upstairs to the bedroom. Jerry followed after her.

"Where have you been all evening? I was worried about you." His tone betrayed his true feelings.

"I told you, I went over to Heather's to help —"

Jerry cut her off. "I called Heather and she said you weren't there — and neither was Phil. Are you and Phil having an affair?"

After a silent moment, she began to cry softly. "Jerry, I'm so sorry. I never meant to hurt you like this. Phil and Heather were having trouble in their marriage, and he needed someone to talk to, and one thing led to another and soon.... Oh, Jerry, I'm so sorry. How will you ever be able to forgive me?"

In a strange way, Jerry was more relieved than outraged by his wife's confession. Not that he wasn't angry and hurt by the betrayal of the two people closest to him. But just as the survivors of terminally ill patients often do their grieving long before the funeral, Jerry had spent the last several weeks troubled over his growing suspicions. Now that everything was out in the open, he and Misty could begin the healing process. Out of sheer will power Jerry uttered the next sentences.

"Misty, there's no way I could ever describe to you how much this hurts me. To think of you cheating on me is bad enough — but with my best friend! I doubt I'll ever get over this completely. But I do love you and believe that God brought us together. I really want to try and salvage our marriage."

Misty didn't utter a word. Maybe, Jerry thought, she was so overwhelmed by his vote of confidence in the relationship that she was speechless. So he continued with increasing conviction.

"I don't think it's any accident that just last week in our men's group we were studying the story of Hosea in the Bible and saw how God told Hosea to take back his adulterous wife. Misty, I love you, and regardless of what you've done, I forgive you and want to make this work."

At this point, Jerry expected Misty to break down into uncontrollable sobs, run into his arms, and express her profound gratitude for his unconditional love. But none of that happened. Instead she continued to cry softly, her head buried in her hands.

"Didn't you hear what I said, Misty? I love you. I forgive you."

Again no response, except that Misty's sobs increased in intensity.

"Misty, you told me you were sorry for hurting me so much. That means you want to end this thing with Phil, don't you?"

With one sentence, Jerry's worst fears were confirmed.

"I don't know what I want right now," Misty answered, gaining her composure. "But I know that our marriage isn't working and I need some time to think."

"Are you saying you plan to keep seeing Phil?"

"I'm saying that I'm not ready to end anything — either with you or with Phil. I don't know what I want."

"But you said just a few minutes ago you were sorry for hurting me. How can you mean that and keep sleeping with my best friend?"

"Jerry, I *am* sorry for the hurt all this is causing you, and I take most of the responsibility for this mess. You have every right to be angry with me, and I wouldn't blame you for a moment if you walked out right now. But I'm asking you to be patient with me. Give me some time to sort out my true feelings. I love you, but I can't promise anything right now."

Now, as Jerry talked with me, he was filled with questions about forgiveness. Although his wife had apologized for her infidelity, was that the same as asking for forgiveness? And even if it was, could Jerry actually forgive her when she had announced her intentions to continue with her affair? Was it possible for Jerry to forgive Misty and still divorce her on the biblical grounds of adultery? And finally, if it was right to give Misty time to "sort out" her true feelings—how much time should Jerry give her?

WANTING TO FEEL FORGIVEN

Nickie Boyd was abandoned by her father and mother when she was a little girl, but her grandparents in North Carolina happily agreed to take her in. Although money was tight for them, Nickie told me about their generosity.

"They gave me anything I wanted. They were cotton-mill people, but if I wanted a Coca-Cola—they cost a nickel—I got it. Comic books were ten cents, and she'd get me two. Saturday morning theater was fifteen cents, and I always got to go."

One of the things Nickie learned growing up was the benefits of forgiveness. "It's something my grandmother taught me," Nickie said. "If you don't forgive others, it will eat you alive."

After her grandfather died in 1964, Nickie began stopping by regularly to care for her grandmother. She cooked, cleaned, and changed her grandmother's clothes and bedsheets. For an eight-year stretch, Nickie visited her grandmother every day without fail—no vacations, no breaks.

One day in late 1994, Nickie arrived at her grandmother's home and discovered that she had fallen. She had to call the fire department for assistance in getting her grandmother back into bed. Alarmed over what might happen in case of a fire and distressed over her inability to adequately care for her grandmother in her worsening health, Nickie finally placed her in a nursing home, despite her grandmother's objections.

Then came a staggering blow. After only three weeks in the nursing home, her grandmother died. "If I hadn't taken her over there," Nickie lamented, "she wouldn't have died."

A few days after the funeral, Nickie's minister came to visit. She related to him the terrible guilt she felt over her grandmother's death. The pastor prayed for Nickie.

"He prayed; I listened," she says, "but I felt no comfort at all."

She continues to ask God for forgiveness, but still has not received the answer she seeks.

"If you're forgiven, you just know," she says. "You feel it. When you're really, really thirsty, it's the first swallow that tastes so good and sweet. That's what forgiveness tastes like. And since she died, I have never tasted that."[1]

FORGIVE EVERYONE?

Chet Hodgin of Jamestown, New York, is a devout Christian who understands what the Bible says about forgiveness. "Christ taught us that it's something we Christians should be willing to do if the offender is asking forgiveness or is repentant for his or her action. Then it becomes our Christian obligation to forgive." But he says he has difficulty agreeing with those who teach that Christians "should offer carte blanche forgiveness for every sin committed against us."

One can sympathize with Hodgin's feelings. In 1992, his son Kevin, a pizza delivery man, was killed in an armed robbery. His other son, Keith, was murdered in 1994 by a man Hodgin had fired from his business.

Since the killers have not repented of their actions, Hodgin feels no obligation to forgive. Would he forgive if the killers ever repented? "I would not necessarily say yes; we'll talk about it when the time comes."

Hodgin has little patience with Christians who want to talk only about his obligation to forgive. He says they give him the impression "that if we as Christians don't forgive everyone who sins against us, then we are equally guilty somehow, and I don't buy that."

Hodgin is channeling some of his rage into developing a support network for crime victims. He says this is something that the church should be doing, but the church seems to be more concerned with "the reconciliation between prisoners and their victims. Well, while the church is worried about redeeming the defendants, I'm concerned with the victims that are lying on the sidewalk, bleeding.... Don't come asking for forgiveness for the people that have killed my children."[2]

WHY THE DISCONNECT?

"Forgiveness," C. S. Lewis once observed, "is a beautiful word, until you have something to forgive." If you've spent any time in church at all, you probably esteem the concept of forgiveness, at least in general. You understand that turning the other cheek is preferable to breaking your offender's jaw. No doubt you've read some of the following verses on the importance of forgiveness:

> If therefore you are presenting your offering at the altar, and there remember that your brother has something against you, leave your offering there before the altar, and go your way; first be reconciled to your brother, and then come and present your offering. (Matthew 5:23-24)

> For if you forgive men for their transgressions, your heavenly Father will also forgive you. But if you do not forgive men, then your Father will not forgive your transgressions. (Matthew 6:14-15)

> Then Peter came and said to Him, "Lord, how often shall my brother sin against me and I forgive him? Up to seven times?" Jesus said to him, "I do not say to you, up to seven times, but up to seventy times seven." (Matthew 18:21-22)

> And whenever you stand praying, forgive, if you have anything against anyone; so that your Father also who is in heaven may forgive you your transgressions. But if you do not forgive, neither will your Father who is in heaven forgive your transgressions. (Mark 11:25-26)

> And be kind to one another, tender-hearted, forgiving each other, just as God in Christ also has forgiven you. (Ephesians 4:32)

You know that forgiveness is a biblical concept. Somewhere along the way you also may have been warned about the physical, emotional, and spiritual consequences of unforgiveness. Most of all, you are genuinely grateful for a God who was willing to take on human form and die an excruciating death that you might be forgiven of *your* sins.

Why, then, is there such a disconnect between our understanding of forgiveness and our willingness to grant it to others?

Respected counselor and author David Seamands may have an answer:

> Many years ago I was driven to the conclusion that the major cause of most emotional problems among evangelical Christians are these: the failure to understand, receive, and live out God's unconditional love, forgive-

> ness, and grace to other people. We read, we hear, we believe a good theology of grace. But that's not the way we live. The good news of the gospel has not penetrated the level of our emotions.[3]

Reading Seamands's quote reminds me of a story about a Sunday school teacher. In the middle of the lesson one Sunday, two boys in the back of the room were arguing. The teacher stopped the class and asked what the problem was. One of the boys replied that on the way to Sunday school the other had hit him.

This is a great opportunity to teach them about forgiveness, the teacher thought. He called the two boys to the front of the class and emphasized how much God wants us to forgive each other. Then the teacher asked the all-important question.

"Brian, will you forgive Luke?"

"Sure," Brian said. He then hauled off and punched Luke in the stomach.

"Wait a minute," the teacher yelled, grabbing Brian by the arm. "I asked you to forgive Luke, not hit him."

"I will forgive him," Brian protested, "but I had to get even with him first."

As C. S. Lewis said — forgiveness is a beautiful word until…

AN ISSUE THAT WON'T GO AWAY

The issue of forgiveness touches us every day and in every way. Sometimes it's a major crisis — like those described in this chapter's opening pages — that forces us to choose between forgiveness and unforgiveness. More often it is lesser offenses that we must deal with, such as:

when our child doesn't receive a coveted invitation to a birthday party
when we aren't selected for a leadership position in the church
when a friend refuses to show the proper amount of concern over our problem
when a coworker spreads a lie that keeps us from receiving a promotion

In my experience as a pastor I've discovered that regardless of the size of the offense, forgiveness is not usually the preferred response. Why is that? Why do we Christians, who have been forgiven so much, have such difficulty forgiving others? Is it because forgiveness has not penetrated beneath the topsoil of our minds to our emotions, as Seamands claims? Perhaps. But I also believe there are other reasons.

You Can't Give What You Don't Have

First, it's hard to impart something to another person that *you* have not fully experienced. My younger daughter is getting ready to celebrate another birthday this weekend, and my wife and I have decided that one of her rites of passage needs to be learning to ride a bicycle without training wheels. Having already gone through the process with one very impatient daughter, I know it won't be easy. But after a few spills, bruised kneecaps, and many tears, she *will* master the skill of bicycling.

How can I be so confident? Did I read some detailed book or attend a seminar on bicycling instruction that qualifies me to be a teacher? No, I learned how from my father. Thirty-seven years ago he patiently walked beside me as I wobbled along our front driveway on my first real bike, always careful to reach out when I began to fall, but making me feel as if I were on my own. And next week as I try to teach that same skill to my daughter, I will imitate my own father's methodology and, hopefully, patience.

If the majority of people on this planet have never experienced the unconditional forgiveness God offers through Jesus Christ, is it any wonder why the majority of people also have difficulty forgiving others? You cannot give away what you don't possess. Or put another way, only the forgiven can truly forgive. We learn how to forgive from our Father. That's why I've devoted the first section of this book to the subject of God's forgiveness. Only after we understand — and experience — our Father's grace are we in a position to extend that grace to others.

And yet if experiencing God's grace were the only requirement for forgiving, it stands to reason that the church would be filled with forgiving people. But that's rarely the case, is it? Some of the most unforgiving people you'll ever encounter are those who occupy a pew with you on Sunday mornings. I remember the words of my former pastor and mentor Dr. W. A. Criswell: "If I ever fall into a sin, I pray that I don't fall into the hands of those censorious, critical, self-righteous judges in the church. I'd rather fall into the hands of the barkeepers, streetwalkers, and dope peddlers, because the church people tend to tear each other apart with their gossipy tongues." What a damning indictment! And yet most of us know it's the truth. Why?

What Is Forgiveness?

A second reason many people, including Christians, find it difficult to forgive is that they don't understand what real forgiveness is...and what it isn't.

For example, I frequently counsel with individuals who would genuinely like to let go of the bitterness they've been harboring for years, but haven't done so because they've been waiting for their offender's repentance or rehabilitation. They've been taught by well-meaning Christians that it's impossible to forgive someone who doesn't first ask for forgiveness. After all, their reasoning goes, we're told to forgive just as Christ has forgiven us. God doesn't offer carte blanche forgiveness to everyone, but only to those who ask for it. How can we demand any less from our offender than the perfect Forgiver requires of us?

Sometimes our misunderstanding of forgiveness is linked with legitimate fears about the consequences of forgiveness. A woman who was physically abused by her husband may be reluctant to forgive her mate because she believes by doing so she would forfeit her physical safety. Two parents may want to forgive a relative for sexually abusing their child but be fearful about their child's safety. If they really forgive, should they simply expect the best and allow their child to be around the relative again? Doesn't the Bible teach that "perfect love casts out fear" (1 John 4:18)?

At other times our lack of understanding about forgiveness leads to illegitimate guilt, and this in turn can make us hesitant to forgive again. A wife forgives her husband for an affair, but every time they start to become intimate, images of his infidelity flash into her mind. By her own reasoning, she must not truly have forgiven her husband. After all, when God forgives, doesn't He forget? He promises, "For I will forgive their iniquity, and their sin I will remember no more" (Jeremiah 31:34). Are forgiveness and forgetting synonymous?

A failure to understand the true nature of forgiveness leads to prolonged bitterness, illegitimate fears, and unnecessary guilt. That's why we'll devote the second part of this book to exposing some of the misunderstandings about forgiveness that keep us from receiving and granting life's most important gift. Specifically we'll examine the relationship between —

forgiveness and repentance
forgiveness and consequences
forgiveness and reconciliation
forgiveness and forgetting

The depth of misunderstanding about these issues comes through loud and clear in a national opinion study commissioned by my publisher in connection with this book. These professional researchers conducted interviews with a representative sampling of adults across the United States, seeking their views on a number of forgiveness-related topics. This included asking for the respondents' perspectives on five forgiveness "myths" that this book addresses. In their resulting report, entitled "Americans' Views on Forgiveness," the researchers analyzed their findings:

> Do most adults have a biblical viewpoint about forgiveness? Do most Christians? The conclusion that emerges from this research is that probably very few Americans (and only a small handful of born-again Christians) have a coherent, biblical worldview on the issue of forgiveness.
>
> For instance, based on the five "myths" about forgiveness that we examined, we discovered that only 4% of respondents gave the biblical response to all five statements. Among born-again Christians, only 5% disagreed with all five of the myths.[4]

The Guilt-Blame Seesaw

A final reason many people find it difficult to forgive is because of the "guilt-blame" seesaw they're riding. Allow me to explain. Travel back to your childhood days and recall what it was like to play with a friend on a seesaw. What happened when a mischievous playmate suddenly scrambled off the seesaw while you were still on the other end? CRASH! The only way you and your partner could ensure a safe landing was to get off the seesaw simultaneously.

Now imagine in your mind a seesaw with one side labeled "guilt" and the other "blame." The only way to keep the seesaw in balance is to make sure you have enough "blame" to balance your "guilt." The more guilt you feel for your own mistakes, the more blame you must pile on to remain in emotional equilibrium. But what happens if you suddenly get rid of the blame toward others (through forgiveness) without also removing your guilt? You will emotionally "crash."

I often play with my daughters on the seesaw at our neighborhood playground, but I've never heard one of them say while suspended in the air, "Dad, get off so I can feel the pain of a sudden fall." Most people I deal with have that same sense of self-preservation. They don't want to grant forgiveness and be left holding the bag of personal guilt. Instead, their own guilt for personal failures in their relationships will prohibit them from forgiving others. If they do choose to forgive, they will attach their blame to someone else.

That's why we will devote the last section of this book to discussing the how-tos of forgiveness — how to receive it and how to grant it to others. We'll even talk about the issue of forgiving God. Does God play any role in the hurts that we have experienced? Shouldn't He be willing to accept *some* of the blame for our pain? I'm convinced that one reason we're hesitant to forgive people is that it is much easier (and safer) to blame others for our problems than to blame the most logical "Culprit." And yet at some point we must confront the question, "Why did God allow this hurt in my life?" In the final chapter we'll address this issue as we examine the most necessary ingredient in the whole process of forgiveness: faith.

LETTING GO OF THE HURT

I'm fairly confident that the reason you went to the time and expense to pick up this book is that somewhere in your past there was a tremendous hurt with which you are still struggling. That hurt might be

an unwanted divorce
termination from your job
a betrayed friendship
sexual abuse you experienced as a child
a slanderous rumor that has robbed you of your reputation

My prayer is that you'll find in the following pages both the encouragement and the practical instruction you need to let go of that hurt — not in order to fulfill some moralistic requirement, but so that you might experience that soul-quenching relief that comes with forgiveness. Lewis Smedes said it best when he observed, "The first and often the only person to be healed by forgiveness is the person who does the forgiveness.... When we genuinely forgive, we set a prisoner free and then discover that the prisoner we set free was us."[5]

CHAPTER 2

The Basis for All Forgiveness

When forgiveness doesn't make sense

Dawn Smith Jordan had to learn about forgiveness the hard way. A few years ago in our church service, she shared with us her dramatic story (which was the basis for a CBS television movie, *Nightmare in Columbia County*).

Dawn told us that on May 31, 1985, her seventeen-year-old sister, Sherrie Smith, was abducted while walking from her car to the mailbox. Five days later Sherrie's body was discovered.

Soon afterward the Smith family received a letter in the mail that had been written by Sherrie. The kidnapper had allowed her to write it before he murdered her, then had mailed her letter.

Sherrie called her letter "my last will and testament." She wrote, "I love you all so much. Please don't let this ruin your lives. Keep living one day at a time for Jesus. Don't worry about me because I know I'm going to be with my Father." Since the time Sherrie and Dawn were little girls, their father had made a practice of taping Scripture verses to the bathroom mirror for them to memorize. Now, in the moment before she was to die, Sherrie recalled one of those verses and wrote, "Everything works out for the good of those who love the Lord. All my love, Sherrie."

But her family's nightmare was far from over. The killer telephoned the Smith family numerous times, cruelly describing the gruesome details of how he had murdered Sherrie.

Ultimately, he was apprehended and received two death sentences for his brutal crime. Now, Dawn thought, the story was finally finished, and she could try and rebuild her shattered life.

A few years later, however, she received a letter that would forever change her life. The killer wrote to Dawn to let her know that he had become a Christian. "Dawn," he asked, "will you and your family ever forgive me for what I have done?"

Stop for a moment and ask yourself how you would respond to that question, if you were in the Smith family's place.

In her testimony to our church, Dawn told us, "I knew as a Christian that when somebody wrongs you, you forgive them. That's basic knowledge. Yet all of a sudden forgiveness was a lot harder to do." In her honest struggle with the forgiveness issue, God brought her to Ephesians 4:32 — "And be kind to one another, tender-hearted, forgiving each other, just as God in Christ also has forgiven you."

"It wasn't easy," Dawn said. "It wasn't overnight. But God gave me the answer that I needed. We are to forgive just as Jesus forgave us. I was finally able to sit down and write a letter to Mr. Bell telling him that only because of the grace that I have received in my life could I let him know that he was forgiven."[1]

THE INSEPARABLE LINK

There is an inseparable link between receiving God's forgiveness and granting forgiveness to others. "Just as God in Christ *also* has forgiven you" is the hinge that relates grace to forgiveness.

Can only Christians forgive? Of course not. Everyday there are non-Christians who choose to let go of offenses as trivial as someone cutting in front of them in traffic or as major as marital infidelity. But the Bible does teach that Christians should find it easier to forgive, given the grace that they have experienced.

Remember the story of when Jesus came to dinner at the home of Simon the Pharisee? While Jesus was there, a woman (most likely a prostitute) crashes Simon's dinner party and approaches Jesus with a vial of expensive perfume.

> And standing behind Him at His feet, weeping, she began to wet His feet with her tears, and kept wiping them with the hair of her head, and kissing His feet, and anointing them with the perfume. (Luke 7:38)

As you can imagine, this causes quite a stir among the guests. Simon, a member of the religious sect that prided itself for keeping the law, is thoroughly disgusted by the woman's presence in his home, not to mention her treatment of Jesus. *If this Jesus were* really *a prophet,* he thinks to himself, *He would know this woman is a prostitute.*

Reading Simon's mind, Jesus decides to have a little fun with His host and at the same time leave no doubt about His own true identity. "Simon," He announces, "I have something to say to you!"

I can just hear Simon stumbling around. "W-w-w-well, say it, Jesus."

Then Jesus gives Simon and the dinner guests a little vignette:

> A certain moneylender had two debtors: one owed five hundred denarii, and the other fifty. When they were unable to repay, he graciously forgave them both. Which of them therefore will love him more? (Luke 7:41-42)

Simon is smart enough to know where this conversation is going. After a moment's hesitation he answers, "I suppose the one whom he forgave more."

Bingo. Simon gets it right. "You have judged correctly," Jesus says. But He has more to tell Simon:

> Do you see this woman? I entered your house; you gave Me no water for My feet, but she has wet My feet with her tears, and wiped them with her hair. You gave Me no kiss; but she, since the time I came in, has not ceased to kiss My feet. You did not anoint My head with oil, but she anointed My feet with perfume. For this reason I say to you, her sins, which are many, have been forgiven, for she loved much; but he who is forgiven little, loves little. (Luke 7:44-47)

Frankly, it's quite easy to make the wrong application from this story. In fact, I'm quite certain that Simon — infected with a serious case of self-righteousness — missed Jesus' point by a mile, since there's no indication he ever became a believer. I can imagine Simon concluding, "I see what You're saying, Jesus. Big sinners have a lot more to be thankful for than little sinners like me. If I were a filthy prostitute like her, I probably would throw myself at Your feet, too. Thank God I'm not in that condition!"

Simon understood only that sinners need forgiveness. Jesus had made that point earlier to a group of Pharisees (perhaps including Simon) who objected to His dining with the tax gatherers and sinners:

> It is not those who are well who need a physician, but those who are sick. I have not come to call the righteous but sinners to repentance. (Luke 5:31-32)

What Simon failed to understand — along with so many others today — was that *he* was among those who were spiritually sick and in need of forgiveness.

WE ALL NEED FORGIVENESS

A number of years ago my mom was diagnosed with colon cancer and told that she had only four months to live. During the final days of her life, a local television station interviewed her about her illness and the courage with which she was facing death. "Mrs. Jeffress," the interviewer asked, "how does it feel to know that that you are terminal?"

"The truth is," my mom quickly answered with her unique combination of wit and wisdom, "we are all terminal. The only difference is that some of us realize it and some of us don't."

That was the only real difference between the prostitute and Simon. Both suffered from the terminal disease of sin. Both were in danger of eternal death. Both were in need of a supernatural healing from the great Physician. The only difference was their awareness of their condition. The streetwalker *understood* her need for forgiveness; Simon *denied* his.

What does this story have to do with forgiving others? Forgiven people are in a better position to extend grace than those who are unforgiven. I'm not suggesting that only Christians can forgive, nor am I claiming that Christians are necessarily more forgiving than non-Christians. But Christians have three distinct advantages that *should* make them better forgivers than unbelievers:

1. Forgiven people understand their own guilt.
2. Forgiven people understand the need for intervention.
3. Forgiven people understand grace.

FORGIVEN PEOPLE UNDERSTAND THEIR OWN GUILT

The primary reason Christians should be better forgivers than non-Christians is that they've been forced to admit their own failures. Simon the Pharisee imagined a wide gap between himself and the prostitute, so he felt contempt for her. After all, he was a religious leader and she was a woman of the night. But this supposed morality gulf between the religious leaders and the common people is something Jesus devoted much of His teaching against. When we realize that the moral gulf between us and our offender is not that significant, we remove a tremendous barrier to forgiveness.

In God's eyes, all of us need forgiveness. God has declared every one of us "guilty" before Him. In God's economy there is no difference between the preacher and the prostitute, the governor and the gunman, or the sophisticate and the savage.

In the book of Romans, which reveals how we can receive God's forgiveness for our sins, the first three chapters are devoted to explaining our guilt before God. The heathen who has never heard the gospel is guilty; the religionist who tries to earn God's approval is guilty; even the Israelite from God's chosen people is guilty. We are all guilty before God, as Paul declares in the climactic verses of this section:

> What then? Are we better than they? Not at all; for we have already charged that both Jews and Greeks are all under sin: as it is written,
> "There is none righteous, not even one;
> There is none who understands,
> There is none who seeks for God;
> All have turned aside, together they have become useless;
> There is none who does good,
> There is not even one."
>
> (Romans 3:9-12)

Did you catch that? "None righteous...not even one...none who understands...none who seeks for God...none who does good." And just in case anyone misses his point, Paul adds these familiar words: "For *all* have sinned and fall short of the glory of God" (Romans 3:23).

Every year at our Vacation Bible School I illustrate this truth to our children by acting out a silly scenario with our minister of education and our minister of music. I have the children imagine the three of us standing on a beach in California. In a moment of insanity, we decide to swim to Hawaii. We all jump in the water at the same time. After the first mile our minister of music gives up and sinks to the bottom; after five miles our minister of education succumbs to exhaustion; but the pastor, being in great physical shape (the kids erupt in laughter at that remark), swims one hundred miles before giving up.

Then I ask the question, "Who made it to Hawaii?" Even though two of us swam farther than the music minister, and I outdistanced the education minister as well, we all fell far short of the beaches of Waikiki and became food for the fish. "For all have sinned and fall short of the glory of God."

Not long ago I read a newspaper story about a father who tortured and then burned to death his four young children. One can hardly imagine a more reprehensible act. Compare that man to a father like Walt Disney who brought laughter and happiness to millions of children around the globe. Both men are fathers, but in our minds a vast gulf separates them. Compared to the holiness of God, however, such differences in human behavior are negligible, according to the apostle Paul. Regardless of our individual virtues, we have all fallen woefully short of the perfection God demands.

Realizing this is not only the foundation for receiving God's forgiveness, but also the basis for extending forgiveness to others.

In *The Gulag Archipelago,* the great Russian writer Aleksandr Solzhenitsyn tells of having befriended an army officer in World War II. Their shared convictions and dreams formed what seemed to be an unbreakable bond. But after the war, they went in opposite directions. Solzhenitsyn was thrown into a Russian gulag for his unrelenting courage. His friend became an interrogator who brutally tortured prisoners in order to gain confessions. How could such a difference be explained between two men who had been so similar? Solzhenitsyn refused to believe that he was totally good and his friend was totally evil. Instead, Solzhenitsyn wrote that the dividing line between good and evil cuts through each of us:

> If only it were all so simple! If only there were evil people...committing evil deeds, and it were necessary only to separate them from the rest of us and destroy them. But the line dividing good and evil cuts through the heart of every human being. And who is willing to destroy a piece of his own heart?
>
> During the life of any heart this line keeps changing place; sometimes it is squeezed one way by exuberant evil and sometimes it shifts to allow enough space for good to flourish. One and the same human being is, at various ages, under various circumstances, a totally different human being. At times he is close to being a devil, at times to sainthood. But his name doesn't change, and to that name we ascribe the whole lot, good and evil.[2]

When we understand that the same evil that motivated our offender to hurt us resides in *our* heart as well, we're in a much better position to forgive.

FORGIVEN PEOPLE UNDERSTAND THE NEED FOR INTERVENTION

One of our greatest barriers to forgiveness is believing that our offender must make the first move. We feel that before we can honestly forgive another person, that person must demonstrate some remorse and desire for reconciliation. But the truth of the matter is that sometimes the offended party must take the first step to restore a fractured relationship.

Several days ago I had to punish one of my daughters for her refusal to obey a simple request. After pronouncing the sentence of no television for several days, she stormed into her room yelling about the unfairness of the whole situation and expressing her strong desire for a new father. Believe me, remorse and repentance were nowhere in sight.

Since I was the one who was wronged, I would have clearly been within my rights to allow her to suffer the consequences of her action — a stalemate in which she stayed in her corner of the house and I in mine. I could have decided not to talk with her until she came to her senses and realized how wrong she was. I'm stronger than she is emotionally, and I could wait her out. It might take hours, days, or possibly months.

But my love for my daughter and desire for reconciliation overshadowed my sense of justice. I went looking for her.

I knocked on her bedroom door. No answer. Quietly turning the doorknob, I entered her room and heard her sobbing uncontrollably. But I couldn't see her anywhere. She had crawled underneath the bed. So I crawled underneath the bed too. After calmly rehearsing her transgressions and why punishment was warranted, I reached over and pulled her close to me and reassured her of my love for her and my willingness to forgive her. In an instant our relationship was restored.

Those who demand repentance from their offender before granting forgiveness often point to Ephesians 4:32 or Colossians 3:13 to defend their position. They say, "The Bible tells us to forgive one another the same way God forgave us. If God demands that we repent of our sins, why shouldn't we insist that our offender show that same kind of remorse before we forgive him?"

Good question, and one that we'll deal with more fully later. But we should never forget that God is the One who always takes the initiative in forgiving. Although He is the offended party, He is also the One who seeks reconciliation with us.

We find this wonderful truth illustrated in the first act of forgiveness recorded in the Bible.

IN THE GARDEN

Genesis 3 is an account of how sin first entered into the world. The serpent, empowered by Satan, seduced the man and woman into eating from the one tree God had made off-limits:

> When the woman saw that the tree was good for food, and that it was a delight to the eyes, and that the tree was desirable to make one wise, she took from its fruit and ate; and she gave also to her husband with her, and he ate. (Genesis 3:6)

God's earlier command to the first couple had been simple: "From any tree of the garden you may eat freely; but from the tree of the knowledge of good and evil you shall not eat, for in the day that you eat from it you shall surely die" (2:16-17). No complicated theology there. Obey and live; disobey and die. Now that Adam and Eve had disobeyed that command, God would have been completely justified in killing them right then and damning their eternal souls. But instead, the remainder of Genesis 3 records God's initiative in reconciliation:

> And they heard the sound of the LORD God walking in the garden in the cool of the day, and the man and his wife hid themselves from the presence of the LORD God

> among the trees of the garden. Then the LORD God called to the man, and said to him, "Where are you?" (3:8-9)

Although Adam and Eve had lost their way, God came searching for them. After explaining the temporal consequences of their actions, He also took the initiative to provide a "covering" for their actions in the form of clothing — "And the LORD God made garments of skin for Adam and his wife, and clothed them" (3:21).

At this point in time Adam and Eve were wearing fig-leaf garments that they had prepared immediately after their sin, when "the eyes of both of them were opened, and they knew that they were naked; and they sewed fig leaves together and made themselves loin coverings" (3:7). By this action they had shown that they sensed their guilt and their need for a covering.

Guilt is indeed one consequence of sin, though I hesitate to use that word because it's too often used as a synonym for an illegitimate emotion to be rooted out of our lives at any cost. Some of the guilt we feel certainly *is* illegitimate; a few years ago I wrote a book about the sources and cure for illegitimate guilt. But the main reason most people feel guilty is because they *are* guilty.

Adam and Eve did not need a preacher to tell them they were guilty of sinning against God. Their transgression motivated them to cover themselves with a pitiful collection of fig leaves as an outward admission of that guilt.

But Adam and Eve needed to recognize another truth before they could clothe themselves with their custom-made garments from God: They had to acknowledge the inadequacy of their self-made covering.

Though the fig-leaf clothing hid the couple's nakedness, it did not remove their shame, which could happen only by the more effective covering God would provide.

In the same way, you and I must first admit our own inadequacies before we can receive God's forgiveness. Although our good works might be useful in hiding the true condition of our souls from others, they're absolutely useless in the sight of God.

James Montgomery Boice compares our good works to Monopoly money. As long as you're only playing Monopoly, those blue fifties and yellow hundreds are of tremendous value. But they're absolutely worthless in the real world. (If you don't believe me, just try sending in a wad of them for your next mortgage payment.) In the same way, our good deeds are like a "filthy garment" (Isaiah 64:6) in the sight of God. In God's economy they're as worthless as play money.

Receiving God's forgiveness requires a realization of our need and of our inadequacy. But note that God required nothing of Adam and Eve before He initiated the reconciliation process. He came looking for them. He prepared the covering before they ever acknowledged their need for a covering. And God does the same for each of us.

Consider these passages that speak of God's initiative in the forgiveness process:

> For while we were still helpless, at the right time Christ died for the ungodly. (Romans 5:6)

> But God, being rich in mercy, because of His great love with which He loved us, even when we were dead in our

> transgressions, made us alive together with Christ. (Ephesians 2:4-5)
>
> In this is love, not that we loved God, but that He loved us and sent His Son to be the propitiation for our sins. (1 John 4:10)

Although repentance is a necessary ingredient to experience God's forgiveness, we should never forget that God has made all the first moves to bring about that reconciliation with His creatures. That's why Christians, above all people, should understand that sometimes the offended party must take the first step to restore a broken relationship. While repentance and remorse are necessary to *receive* forgiveness, they are not prerequisites for *granting* forgiveness.

FORGIVEN PEOPLE UNDERSTAND GRACE

Several decades ago, at a British conference on comparative religions, a group of experts were discussing the uniqueness of Christianity. What differentiates Christianity from other religions? When C. S. Lewis entered the room and was told that the group was trying to ascertain the unique element of Christianity, he remarked, "Oh, that's easy. It's grace." After more discussion, the participants agreed. The idea of God's love coming free of charge, no strings attached, is a novel idea. Every other religion emphasizes man's responsibility to secure God's approval. Only Christianity makes God's love unconditional.[3]

But what is grace? Take a moment to think of a definition in your own words. With that definition in mind, can you recall an instance when you were the recipient of grace from another person? And can you think of a time when you extended grace to another person — and how that made you feel?

Here's my definition: *Grace is a deliberate decision to give something good to someone who doesn't deserve it.*

At some time in your life you've probably been the recipient of this kind of grace. For example, credit-card holders benefit from a "grace period." Although your creditor has the right to demand immediate payment for the debt you've incurred, he gives you twenty-five days of freedom from that obligation. (After that, unfortunately, the meter starts running.) Maybe you can recall an instance when a teacher extended grace to you by delaying a test or the due date for a project, or a time when you received a "warning" instead of a ticket for an obvious traffic violation.

Not long ago a woman shared with me that her husband had been engaged in a yearlong affair. Though she had biblical grounds to divorce him, she chose not to exercise that option and instead was determined to rebuild her marriage. She gave her undeserving husband a second chance.

The basis for all grace is God's offer to release us from the consequences of our sin. Although we deserve eternal punishment for our transgressions against God, He offers to free us from that punishment and to give us eternal life in return.

But such an action is not without cost. Grace does not mean that God simply overlooks our sin, as I might choose to ignore a smart-aleck answer or disobedient act from one of my children. God's holy nature will not allow Him to simply ignore our sin. "I will not acquit the guilty," God says in Exodus 23:7. "The LORD will by no means leave the guilty unpunished" (Nahum 1:3).

So how can a righteous God extend grace without violating His own nature? If God does not demand that I pay for my sin, then someone else must pay. If God does not hold me responsible for my transgressions, He must hold someone else responsible.

That person is Jesus Christ, who bore our sins through an action that theologians call imputation. The apostle Paul explains it in 2 Corinthians 5:21—

> He made Him who knew no sin to be sin on our behalf,
> that we might become the righteousness of God in Him.

These words speak of the most amazing transaction in history, and they refer to two exchanges that took place on the cross.

First, Jesus Christ assumed the obligation for our sin. He "knew no sin," but God made Him "to be sin on our behalf." This does not mean that Jesus became a sinner, but simply that He paid the obligation for our transgressions.

Philip Yancey recounts a scene in the movie *The Last Emperor* in which the brother of the young emperor of China asks, "What happens when you do wrong?"

"When I do wrong, someone else is punished," the boy emperor replies. To demonstrate his words, he breaks a jar, then has one of his many servants beaten.[4]

But what God has done is a reversal of that pattern. As His subjects, we have all erred, but God in the person of Jesus Christ received the punishment due each one of us.

Even more amazing is the second exchange in the transaction that God performed — the exchange represented by Paul's words, "that we might become the righteousness of God."

When I become a Christian, not only does God place my sin upon Christ, but He then takes the righteousness of Christ and credits it to my spiritual bank account and "justifies" me (the term means "to declare not guilty"). Paul wrote in Romans 4:5,

> But to the one who does not work, but believes in Him who justifies the ungodly, his faith is reckoned as righteousness.

This word "reckoned" is an accounting term that means "to place to someone's account." When I trust in Christ as my Savior, God not only credits Christ with my sin, but He credits me with all the righteousness of Christ.

Imagine that you want to purchase a certain home. The only problem is that your financial statement is in horrendous shape. You lost your job several months ago, you're deeply in debt, and you only have two dollars in your bank account. No banker in his right mind would lend you the money for a new home. That's the bad news.

The good news is that Bill Gates is your father. And his financial statement looks great! Dear old dad, seeing your dilemma, tells you, "I would love to help you out. I will assume the responsibility for your debt. When you go in and see the bank officer tomorrow, instead of submitting your financial statement, use mine."

How would you respond to such an offer? If you were filled with pride (and incredible stupidity), you might say, "Forget it, Dad. I don't need your help. I'll take my chances with the bank and see what they say."

Or you could say, "Dad, I need your help. I've made some bad decisions and I'm practically bankrupt. So I'll accept your generous offer."

You go to the bank the next morning and submit your loan request along with your father's financial statement. Your application for a new home is based on his resources, not your own. And his billions are more than sufficient to cover your mortgage.

That simple scenario illustrates the most profound truth in the universe. God's universal law demands that if you're going to secure a home in heaven you must be perfect. Your goodness must equal that of Jesus Christ. The problem is that we're all morally and spiritually bankrupt. You may have more righteousness in your spiritual bank account than I do, and I may possess more than Adolf Hitler, but it doesn't matter. None of us has enough.

But God has extended to us a gracious offer: "If you would like, I will consider your application for heaven based on My Son's spiritual resources rather than your own. And His righteousness is more than enough to make up for your deficiency."

Amazingly, most people reject God's offer. But those who accept God's invitation are in the best position to understand what grace is all about — granting to others what they do not deserve, earn, or sometimes even request.

On the morning of December 1, 1997, a dozen students gathered to pray as they usually did before the beginning of classes at the Heath High School in Paducah, Kentucky. As they closed their prayer time, a fourteen-year-old freshman approached the prayer group and, without provocation, began shooting into the prayer circle. Three students died and five others were seriously wounded. For weeks, parents, school officials, and the media were at a loss to explain such a vile act.

But many were equally astounded by the willingness of many of the survivors and family members of the deceased to forgive the shooter and his family. One of the survivors was fifteen-year-old Melissa

Jenkins, who expects to spend the rest of her life as a paraplegic because of spinal cord damage from the shooting. And yet Melissa, a Christian, sent this message through a friend to the one who had destroyed her life: "Tell him I forgive him."[5]

Obviously not all Christians are like Melissa Jenkins. Even though they may have come to terms with their own sin, pled for God's intervention, and experienced the grace transaction firsthand, they still refuse to extend that same grace to others.

What are the consequences of this "ungrace"? The answers are the focus of our next chapter.

CHAPTER 3

FORGIVENESS ON TRIAL

Three strong arguments against forgiving others

I'm convinced that too many pastors and Christian authors are closed-minded about this thorny issue of forgiveness. They're prone to tell only one side of the story and lack the objectivity to deal honestly with this most difficult issue.

You want evidence to support my criticism, you say? Fine. When is the last time you heard a sermon or read a book that made a strong case *against* forgiveness? Can you recall hearing of a respected spiritual advisor who counseled a victim of abuse or hurt by saying to that victim, "What happened to you is so awful that you would be a fool to forgive. A lifetime of bitterness is your only reasonable response"?

That's what I thought. You've probably never heard a good argument against forgiveness, and so I want to make such a case through a true story recounted by Lewis Smedes in *Forgive and Forget.*

Simon Wiesenthal was a Jewish architect incarcerated in a Nazi concentration camp in World War II. One day Wiesenthal was on a work detail to a local hospital where wounded German soldiers were treated. A nurse ordered him to follow her to a patient's room. There Wiesenthal was seated beside the bed of a man with his head wrapped in bandages, a young SS trooper whose name was Karl. He gripped Wiesenthal's hand and told him that before he died he had a confession that must be made to a Jew.

Karl told him that on the Russian front he had fought in a village where two hundred Jews were captured. Karl's squad was ordered to plant cans of gasoline in a vacant house, then herd the Jewish men, women, and children inside. They were to ignite the gasoline and shoot anyone who tried to flee.

The prisoners were packed so tightly into the house that they could barely move. The soldiers threw grenades through the windows, and the house erupted in flames.

Karl recalled looking up through a second-floor window to see a man with his clothing on fire. He held a small child in his arms, and beside him stood a woman. With his free hand the man covered the child's eyes, then jumped to the street. Seconds later, the mother followed. But Karl and his fellow soldiers obeyed orders.

"We shot…," he groaned. "Oh, God…I shall never forget — it still haunts me."

Karl continued, "I know that what I have told you is terrible. I have longed to talk about it to a Jew and beg forgiveness from him. I know that what I am asking is almost too much, but without your answer I cannot die in peace."

In his book *The Sunflower,* Wiesenthal recalled his response: "I stood up and looked in his direction, at his folded hands. At last I made up my mind and without a word I left the room."

Throughout the remainder of his life, Wiesenthal struggled with his decision. Should he have forgiven the repentant Nazi? Or are some crimes too heinous to ever be forgiven? Wiesenthal wrestled with those questions and ended the story by asking his readers, "What would you have done?"[1]

What would have been your response had you been in Wiesenthal's place? If the answer "Forgive" comes a little too easily, imagine that the person confessing to you is detailing the murder of *your* children, not those of a stranger.

Do some offenses fall outside the circle of grace?

Are there some wrongs that cannot be absolved through a simple "I'm sorry. Please forgive me"?

Are there times when forgiving is too much to ask from a hurting victim?

I believe Wiesenthal's story illustrates and underscores the four most logical arguments against forgiveness.

"Forgiveness Denies the Seriousness of Sin"

Many people believe that forgiveness is tantamount to denying the severity of an offense — "If I forgive, it's the same as saying that what the offender did wrong does not really matter."

Most of those who think that way would probably still agree that some offenses are so petty that we should overlook them — a forgotten birthday, an interrupted sentence, an unreturned phone call. Solomon wisely counseled us with these words: "The beginning of strife is like letting out water, so abandon the quarrel before it breaks out" (Proverbs 17:14); "A man's discretion makes him slow to anger, and it is his glory to overlook a transgression" (Proverbs 19:11).

Not that small slights aren't painful at times. Think of it this way: One of the occupational hazards of my profession is paper cuts. Let me assure you that the blood is plentiful and the pain is real. But I have a choice of how to deal with those kinds of nicks. I could go to the emergency room of the local hospital and have a doctor examine my injury, disinfect the wound, and bandage my finger. Such a procedure could cost hundreds of dollars and several hours of time. Or I can choose to take care of the problem myself with a ten-cent Band-Aid.

As Solomon explains, a wise person is one who doesn't make a federal case out of every injury in life. Instead he covers over his hurt with the grace of understanding that everyone makes mistakes.

However, is it wise to treat every offense that way? If I counsel a mother to overlook the sexual abuse she suffered as a child the same way I tell a friend to overlook the sarcastic remark of a coworker, am I not trivializing the woman's pain and minimizing the seriousness of incest? Some offenses are so serious that they cannot be overlooked any more than God can overlook our sin.

This may come as a shock to some of you, but do you realize that it's impossible for God to excuse your sin? One of the greatest misconceptions about salvation is to believe that God tells us, "What you did was bad, but I love you so much that we'll forget this ever happened." A holy God is incapable of such an action. Remember again what Scripture says about this: "The LORD will by no means leave the guilty unpunished," and "I will not acquit the guilty" (Nahum 1:3; Exodus 23:7). God does not declare out of the blue that sinners are suddenly righteous and serious offenses are suddenly inconsequential. God's mercy cannot override His holiness. Offenses demand payment.

If a perfect God finds it impossible to summarily dismiss sin against Him, why do we think we could ever overlook the serious hurts inflicted by others? Sin creates an obligation and someone has to pay. Whatever forgiveness is, it should not be confused with glossing over the seriousness of a wrong.

"Forgiveness Lets People Off the Hook Too Easily"

One of the most basic hindrances to forgiveness is the fear of further abuse. We have a legitimate concern that forgiving our offender will give him permission to hurt us even more deeply. An employer who chooses to retain an embezzling subordinate wonders whether he's opening himself up to even greater loss. A wife who forgives an abusive husband fears that she's inviting more beatings. A husband who forgives an adulterous wife is worried about setting himself up for further betrayal.

Such a legitimate fear about the consequences of forgiveness was probably what prompted Peter to ask Jesus, "Lord, how often shall my brother sin against me and I forgive him? Up to seven times?" (Matthew 18:21).

Our immediate response to the apostle's question might be, "Peter, don't be stupid. Don't you realize there's no limit to forgiveness?" But before coming down too hard on Peter, ask yourself, "How many times am I willing to forgive a person for committing the same serious offense against me?" Suddenly, Peter's suggestion of seven times seems quite generous.

This is especially true given the culture in which Peter lived. A popular rabbi of the day taught that you forgive people three times, but the fourth time you refuse. Peter was offering more than twice the going rate of grace, but he still believed there surely must be *some* limit to forgiveness to prevent ourselves from being taking advantage of. To be honest, most of us probably believe the same way.

"FORGIVENESS PLACES TOO MUCH RESPONSIBILITY ON THE VICTIM"

Some people argue quite convincingly that asking victims to let go of their pain and desire for justice is placing too much responsibility on the *offended* instead of the *offender*. It's like coming across the mangled victim of an automobile accident lying near death on the pavement and telling him to take care of his own injuries.

One counseling office gave the following advice to victims of incest:

> Dear Victim:
>
> If you are like most victims who have been sexually abused, you are asking many questions of yourself. We have all heard the old favorites from sex offenders, family members, ministers, and clergy: "Forgive and forget; let bygones be bygones; let's bury the hatchet and start over." These statements seem to encourage victims to feel as though it is their responsibility to take action regarding resolution and forgiveness. This seems strange, since victims are innocent and not responsible for what occurred.... We believe you as a victim are innocent, and we demand restitution be paid to you in some form. You will learn that your rehabilitation is our goal. You are not responsible for the sexual abuse, and you are not responsible for forgiveness. Your sexual offender is responsible for both these things.[2]

Not only is it unfair to place the forgiveness burden on a victim, some say, but it's also unrealistic. Is it logical to expect an incest victim to ever forget what happened to her? Can a wife ever simply press the "delete" key and remove from her memory the pain of an adulterous mate? Should an employee, unfairly terminated six months before eligibility for his pension, be expected to conclude, "What happened to me was bad, but I'll get over it"? When we ask people to let go of such serious hurts, aren't we asking them to do the impossible?

We'll deal with some of these objections to forgiveness in subsequent chapters, but it might be helpful to remember that God doesn't exempt us from tasks just because they're unfair or difficult. For example, consider these famous words of Jesus from the Sermon on the Mount:

> You have heard that it was said, "An eye for an eye, and a tooth for a tooth." But I say to you, do not resist him who is evil; but whoever slaps you on your right cheek, turn to him the other also. And if anyone wants to sue you, and take your shirt, let him have your coat also. And whoever shall force you to go one mile, go with him two. (Matthew 5:38-41)

Notice that in each situation that Jesus mentions here, He places responsibility not on the offender, but on the offended. The offended is to turn the other cheek, offer his coat as well as his shirt, and walk the second mile.

"Forgiveness Is Unjust"

Perhaps the bottom-line argument on which all other objections to forgiveness rests is the belief that forgiveness is unfair. All of us are created in the image of God and regardless of how badly that image has been marred, we still retain a residue of innate fairness. When we see a wrong committed, we know it's unjust for that wrong to go unpunished. In Dostoyevsky's *The Brothers Karamazov,* one of the characters relates to his brother the following incident. A landlord was irritated by a small boy who kept throwing small rocks at his dogs. In order to teach the peasants of the village to respect his property, the landlord forced the little boy's mother to watch while he loosed a pack of his vicious dogs on her little son. The dogs tore the boy's body into bloody pieces while the mother looked on in horror.[3]

Could the landlord ever be forgiven such a wicked action? Who would be in a position to forgive the landlord? And if by some miracle, the mother of the murdered boy could find it in her heart to forgive the landlord, wouldn't there still be something fundamentally unfair in letting the landlord go free without any consequences?

UNDERSTANDING FORGIVENESS

All these rational objections arise from a basic misunderstanding of the concept of forgiveness. Before we define the word, let's understand what forgiveness is *not.*

Forgiveness is not denying the reality of our pain. To ask someone to simply forget a wrong is like asking a person who has lost both arms to pass the ketchup. He can't do it!

Forgiveness is not letting our offender off the hook. Even when we choose to forgive, such forgiveness does not necessarily erase the consequences of our offender's actions.

Forgiveness is not unfair. To forgive another person does not necessitate violating some cosmic rule of justice requiring that every offense must be punished. For God to require us to do something unfair would violate His nature. "There is no injustice with God, is there?" the apostle Paul exclaims. "May it never be!" (Romans 9:14).

If forgiveness is "none of the above," then what is it?

The Greek word translated "forgive" carries the idea of a release from some type of an obligation. Sometimes it referred to the release from a marriage or a job. But the most common use of the word related to release from a financial obligation. That's how Jesus most often illustrated the concept of forgiveness.

Remember the example Jesus used with Simon the Pharisee on the night the prostitute crashed Simon's dinner party?

> A certain moneylender had two debtors: one owed five hundred denarii, and the other fifty. When they were unable to repay, he graciously forgave them both." (Luke 7:41-42)

The moneylender chose to release both of the debtors from their very real obligations. The money owed was not a figment of the lender's imagination. He had two promissory notes in his vault, signed by the borrowers, indicating that he had a right to be paid five hundred and fifty denarii respectively (a denarius was approximately one day's wages).

Notice that in both cases

1. The lender had a legal right to be repaid.
2. The borrowers had an obligation to pay.
3. There was a deficit between the borrowers' debt and the borrowers' resources.

For a moment, let's look at those first two realities. Nowhere in

Jesus' brief example is there any indication that the lender was unreasonable in expecting to be repaid. Although the borrowers could not repay their debt, the lender was the "innocent party" in this situation. Second, the rule of accounting demanded that "the books be balanced." There was a debt on record that had to be satisfied by someone.

Perhaps the greatest misunderstanding about forgiveness is that it is simply an overlooking of another's transgression. Just as we saw that God is incapable of simply sweeping our sin under some divine doormat, so it is impossible to simply excuse the serious wrongs of others. The truth is that someone always has to pay. Why? Because an offense always creates an obligation that must be satisfied.

Imagine that you're stopped at a red light and BAM! — someone rear-ends you. Startled, you get out of the car and inspect the damage. Fortunately, there doesn't appear to be anything seriously wrong with your car. The other driver pours out his apologies, offering to give you the name of his insurance agent. Feeling especially magnanimous, you say, "Forget it," and drive off. You have overlooked his offense.

The next day you begin to notice a strange rattle in the rear end of your car and feel your car pulling strongly to the right. You take the car to your local garage and the mechanic informs you that yesterday's accident inflicted some serious damage to your car — about two thousand dollars' worth.

Who is going to pay for the repairs? Not the other driver — you let him off the hook. And not the mechanic, since he isn't prone to doing charity work. There is only one other person left to pay: YOU.

My point is that the offense (being rear-ended) created an obligation (the cost of repairing the car) that had to be satisfied.

Now let's rewind our melodrama to the moment when you got out to inspect the damage to your car. In this revised version of the story, you immediately notice a huge dent in your rear bumper. You realize it will cost big bucks to repair the damage. But this time the driver is a little old lady who's in tears over the accident. Between sobs she explains that she's a retired missionary and has limited resources and no insurance. "What am I going to do?" she laments.

You tell her to forget it; you will take care of the damage.

The next day you take the car to the mechanic who informs you that it will cost two thousand dollars to repair the car, and you pay the bill.

For the damage the woman caused, there was a deficit between her obligation to pay and her resources to pay. So you decided to cover the deficit yourself.

Notice that here again the financial obligation did not suddenly evaporate. The mechanic did not say, "Oh, it was a missionary who hit you? Well, then, forget it. I'll be happy to fix your car for free." There was still an obligation that you willingly covered.

That story illustrates the essence of forgiveness. When we forgive:

1. We acknowledge a wrong has occurred.
2. We recognize that the wrong has created an obligation for repayment.
3. We choose to release our offender from that obligation and to cover the loss ourselves.

Most of us have little problem with acknowledging when we've been wronged. The majority of us are excellent record keepers and can tell you to the nth decimal point how much someone owes us for their offense against us. The stumbling point for most of us is that third ingredient of forgiveness. Why should I release someone of his obligation to me and suffer the consequences myself?

THE CASE FOR FORGIVENESS

So far we've explored some very logical arguments against forgiveness. But are there equally convincing reasons to unilaterally forgive another person? When everyone around me and everything inside me tells me that I need to cling to a wrong until my offender "pays in full," why should I suddenly let go of his obligation?

Jesus' answer to Peter's question anticipated such objections to forgiveness. When Peter was voluntarily raising the forgiveness limit to seven (and feeling rather self-righteous about it, I'm sure), Jesus astounded Peter and the rest of the crowd by saying, "I do not say to you, up to seven times, but up to seventy times seven" (Matthew 18:22).

After a brief but dramatic pause to allow the impact of His statement to settle in His listeners' minds, Jesus then related a quite dramatic story, which we read in Matthew 18:23-34. Here's the *Reader's Digest* version: A king, suffering a serious cash-flow problem, decides to call in his accounts receivable. He logically begins with the person who owes him the most, a slave who has an outstanding debt of "ten thousand talents." (Since a single talent represented sixty to eighty pounds of silver or gold, we're talking about upwards of five billion dollars in today's currency; you can only imagine the terror the slave felt when the king said, "Pay up!")

Although the slave has no way to make even the smallest dent in such a debt, he offers to repay everything. Can you imagine a more pitiful sight than his begging for just a little more time to repay a five-billion-dollar debt? In a display of uncharacteristic mercy, the king feels compassion for the slave and releases him from his debt.

In that opening scene from the story, we see a perfect illustration of forgiveness. The slave owed a very real debt to the king. The king had every right to expect repayment. But the king voluntarily released the slave of his obligation and covered the loss of the canceled obligation himself. Why was the king willing to do such a thing?

Jesus said that it was because the king felt "compassion." Perhaps the king was able to put himself in the slave's sandals for a moment. Or maybe the king remembered an instance many years earlier when someone had extended grace to him.

Compassion was the king's stated motivation for forgiveness, but may I suggest some other strong reasons for choosing forgiveness?

FORGIVENESS IS OFTEN THE ONLY WAY TO SETTLE A DEBT

The slave owed a debt that he could not possibly repay in a thousand lifetimes. So what alternative to forgiveness did the king have?

"Well," you say, "he didn't have to release the slave; he could have imprisoned him. That would have been a just punishment." True enough. But would the slave's imprisonment have resulted in even one dollar returning to the king's coffers? Was there any advantage to demanding that the slave remain behind bars for the rest of his life? The king was astute enough to realize that he was holding an uncollectible account receivable. No matter how much the slave suffered, the king was going to take a financial bath.

Many people today are struggling with forgiveness because they are unaware that the "debt" they hold is really worthless. They mistakenly believe that there's some payment they can extract from their offender that will compensate for their loss. Understandably, they want vengeance. But the truth is that very few sinners have the resources to pay for their offenses. What satisfactory payment could someone offer you to compensate for

a child killed by a drunk driver
a reputation slandered by a false rumor

a marriage destroyed by infidelity
a childhood innocence stolen by an immoral relative

I often think of Gandhi's observation that the rule of "an eye for an eye, a tooth for a tooth cannot sustain itself forever; ultimately both parties end up blind and toothless."[4] I believe that's why Jesus offered a solution that at first glance appears outlandish, but on closer examination seems more reasonable:

> You have heard that it was said, "An eye for an eye, and a tooth for a tooth." But I say to you, do not resist him who is evil; but whoever slaps you on your right cheek, turn to him the other also. (Matthew 5:38-39)

Like the king in the parable, Jesus understood that forgiveness is sometimes the only way to break the endless cycle of hurt and unfairness, especially in situations where our offender can never make a satisfactory payment for his wrongs.

FORGIVENESS FREES US TO GET ON WITH OUR LIFE

I've made a number of financial mistakes in my life, but my greatest misjudgment has been getting involved in business partnerships with friends. A few years ago a good friend of mine presented me with a "spectacular opportunity" to double my money within six months, and I invested a rather large amount of money in his venture. As you might have predicted, the deal did not deliver what my friend promised. Feeling badly about the situation, he promised to return my money "in a week." A week passed, no check. Two weeks, still no money. Whenever I dropped by his office, he would always be in a meeting. My phone calls went unreturned. Every day for six months, I would anxiously go to the mailbox, looking for the promised check.

One day it dawned on me that I was much more concerned about my friend's obligation than he was. I thought of comedian Buddy Hackett's comment: "I've had a few arguments with people, but I never carry a grudge. You know why? While you're carrying a grudge, they're out dancing." I began to ask myself, "Why do I want to be a financial *and* emotional hostage to this guy?"

So I called my friend and said, "I know you've been avoiding me for months. I understand that you're probably in no position to pay me back the money you promised. So as far as I'm concerned, you don't owe me anything. Let's rebuild our friendship." Admittedly, my motivation for forgiving my friend's debt was primarily selfish. I was ready to get on with my life and be free from my daily mailbox vigil, wondering "Will this be the day?"

I think the king in Jesus' parable may have had a similar motivation in forgiving the slave. He had too many responsibilities in running a kingdom to allow himself to be distracted by one slave's obligation. If the king was always checking with the royal bookkeeper on the status of the slave's debt, he risked neglecting some of his more pressing duties. Since the slave could never repay the debt anyway, why not go ahead and cut his losses rather than risk needless preoccupation with a hopeless situation?

One of the best reasons for forgiving someone is not what it does for them, but what it does for us. As someone once said, letting go of a rattlesnake might help the snake, but it benefits you as well.

I realize that such an argument for forgiveness seems self-serving. And yet God's Word tells us that we need to free ourselves from anything that would distract us from serving Christ:

> Therefore, since we have so great a cloud of witnesses surrounding us, let us also lay aside every encumbrance, and the sin which so easily entangles us, and let us run with endurance the race that is set before us, fixing our eyes on Jesus, the author and perfecter of faith. (Hebrews 12:1-2)

FORGIVENESS IS AN ANTIDOTE TO NEEDLESS SUFFERING

In the opening scene of the story Jesus told in response to Peter's forgiveness question, the king was the central character in this drama. But then Jesus shifted his audience's attention to the unforgiving slave.

Can you imagine the relief that slave must have felt as he left the palace realizing his five-billion-dollar burden had just been lifted? I'm sure he repeatedly rehearsed the king's words: "You are *FORGIVEN*.... You *ARE* forgiven.... *YOU* are forgiven."

But suddenly an alien thought enters his mind. "Debt? Money? Come to think of it, there's someone who owes *me* some money too." A fellow slave owed him about sixteen dollars in today's currency. So he chases down his friend and demands repayment.

"I don't have the money right now," the friend promises, "but if you're patient, I'll repay you."

Sound familiar? These are exactly the words the first slave had spoken to the king. But unlike the king, the slave had no compassion on his fellow slave. He "threw him in prison until he should pay back what was owed" (Matthew 18:30).

When the king heard what the forgiven slave had done, he was outraged. How could someone who had been forgiven so much refuse to forgive so little? The king, "moved with anger, handed him over to the torturers until he should repay all that was owed him" (Matthew 18:34).

Then Jesus added the zinger:

> So shall My heavenly Father also do to you, if each of you does not forgive his brother from your heart. (Matthew 18:35)

Strong words. Is Jesus teaching that God is some sadist who enjoys inflicting pain on His children who refuse to forgive? Of course not. But those who refuse to forgive enter their own private torture chamber. They sentence themselves to a lifetime of needless pain.

In *The Freedom and Power of Forgiveness,* John MacArthur vividly describes the results of unforgiveness:

> Unforgiveness is a toxin. It poisons the heart and mind with bitterness, distorting one's whole perspective on life. Anger, resentment, and sorrow begin to overshadow and overwhelm the unforgiving person — a kind of soul-pollution that enflames evil appetites and evil emotions.[5]

The Bible has a term for unforgiveness: *bitterness.* The Greek word translated "bitter" comes from a word meaning "sharp" or "pointed." Just as there are certain tastes and smells that are "sharp" to the senses, all of us can recall offenses committed against us that may have occurred years ago but still hurt us when we turn them over in our mind. Those who refuse to let go of offenses risk poisoning their own lives and the lives of others around them. That is why the writer of Hebrews warns:

> See to it that no one comes short of the grace of God;
> that no root of bitterness springing up causes trouble, and
> by it many be defiled. (Hebrews 12:15)

With every offense comes a choice. Through God's supernatural enabling we can let go of someone's offense and become better, or we can hold on to that offense and become bitter. The choice is ours. Letting go promotes healing; holding on ensures infection.

James Garfield had been president of the United States for less than four months when he was shot in the back with a revolver on July 2, 1881. While the president remained conscious, the doctor probed the wound with his little finger, unsuccessfully trying to detect the bullet. Over the course of the summer, teams of doctors tried to locate the bullet. The president clung to life through July and August, but in September he finally died — not from the gunshot wound but from infection. The repeated probing of the wound, which the doctor thought would help the president, ultimately killed him.

Continually reliving hurts we've experienced infects not only our life, but the lives of those around us. One of the strongest arguments for forgiveness is the consequences of unforgiveness. Frederick Buechner has written:

> Of the Seven Deadly Sins, anger is possibly the most fun. To lick your wounds, to smack your lips over grievances long past, to roll over your tongue the prospect of bitter confrontations still to come, to savor to the last tooth-

> some morsel both the pain you are given and the pain you are giving back—in many ways it is a feast fit for a king. The chief drawback is that what you are wolfing down is yourself. The skeleton at the feast is you.[6]

FORGIVENESS IS THE OBLIGATION OF THE FORGIVEN

Throughout the Bible there seems to be an inseparable link between receiving and granting forgiveness. In Jesus' story, even the other pagan slaves who served in the king's palace realized that link. They were astounded that someone who had been forgiven so much would refuse to forgive so little, and it was by their report that the king learned about the first slave's refusal to forgive.

When we read this parable, it's apparent that the king represents God and that the first slave represents us. The Bible teaches that our sin against God has produced an obligation we could never hope to repay. Trying to pay for our sin through good works or religious ritual is just as futile as a slave trying to repay a five-billion-dollar debt! It can't be done. But just as the king was moved with compassion by the slave's predicament, God was moved by our hopeless situation and sent Christ to die for us.

But the interaction between the two slaves represents our relationship to those who wrong us. The second slave was indebted to the first slave — no dispute there. The first slave had every right to collect his sixteen dollars. No court would argue otherwise. But Jesus' point was that the first slave had an obligation to release his friend from his debt, considering the debt from which he had just been freed. *Forgiveness is the obligation of the forgiven.*

As I mentioned earlier, I imagine that one reason you picked up this book is because somewhere in your past there's a hurtful experience from which you haven't yet fully recovered. It may be the abandonment by a mate, the betrayal of a friend, or an injury by a stranger. I don't want to discount for even a moment the reality of your anguish. But listen carefully to what Jesus is saying in this story. While the pain someone has inflicted on you is real, it is also negligible compared to the wrong you have committed against God. The difference between another person's sin against you and your sin against God is the difference between sixteen dollars and five billion dollars!

Forgiveness is the obligation of the forgiven.

Part Two

Removing the Forgiveness Barriers

CHAPTER 4

FORGIVENESS AND REPENTANCE

Why the words "I'm sorry" are highly overrated

Forgiveness is the obligation of the forgiven — and *we* are the forgiven. But what about those who never ask for our forgiveness? Should they expect to receive it? Should we be required to give it?

Marla and her family recently moved to a new town. She and her husband were understandably concerned about their grade-school children being able to establish new friendships. Marla did all she could to foster good relationships with other mothers in her neighborhood: inviting them over to coffee, remembering their children's birthdays, volunteering to help with school projects. She even confided in several of them about the difficulty her children were having finding new friends.

One day Marla learned that several of those same neighborhood mothers had organized a slumber party the previous Friday night and had invited most of the neighborhood children, except hers. First,

Marla was hurt, but the hurt soon turned to anger. How could a group of mothers be so cruel, especially when they knew how painful the experience would be to her children? Marla wrestled with whether to confront the women, and risk being further ostracized, or to let it go. But could she honestly forgive these women without first hearing the words "I'm sorry"?

Clint hated confrontations of any kind, but the longer he allowed his partner's anger to fester, the greater the potential risk to their company.

"Jason, I realize that you and I differ over the McKenzie contract, but blowing up at me in front of the other employees yesterday was no way to resolve this issue. It embarrassed me, and it also fueled rumors throughout the company that we're about to dissolve our partnership. In the future I would appreciate your talking to me in private about our disagreements."

There! Clint had said what needed to be said, and he was already feeling better. But Clint was totally unprepared for his partner's response.

"Just who do you think you are, talking to me that way? We're equal partners in this business, and if I have a problem I'll talk to you any way I want to, any *time* I want. And as far as the other employees are concerned, **** them. I don't work for them, they work for me!"

All Clint wanted was to bring closure to this run-in and to get on with operating the company. But could he forgive someone who refused to acknowledge a serious mistake? And even if he was able to forgive Jason, could their relationship ever be salvaged?

Sara has wrestled for years with the guilt and pain of an incestuous relationship with her uncle that began when she was five and continued through her early teen years. She has been divorced twice and in therapy for as long as she can remember. Recently, she heard a series of messages in her church about forgiveness. The pastor shared the three ingredients necessary to initiate a "forgiveness transaction":

1. The offender and the offended acknowledge that a wrong has occurred.
2. The offender repents of his sin.
3. The offended party voluntarily releases the offender from his obligation.

This all made sense to Sara, except for one problem. Her uncle was dead. How can a dead person "acknowledge a wrong" or "repent of his sin"? Are Sara's chances for emotional healing doomed by the fact that her uncle went to his grave without ever asking her forgiveness?

These three scenarios illustrate one of the most frequently cited barriers to forgiveness: the need for repentance. Is repentance a requirement for granting forgiveness to others? Can you honestly and effectively forgive someone who

is *unaware* that he's hurt you
is *unmoved* by the fact that he's offended you
is *unwilling* to admit his mistake
is *unable* to ask forgiveness because of illness or death

The forgiveness "experts" are divided on this issue. Let's allow several of them to make the best argument they can muster *against* unilateral forgiving. One Christian counselor writes:

> Jesus didn't teach unconditional forgiveness in Luke 17. He said, "If your brother sins against you, rebuke him; and if he repents, forgive him. And if he sins against you seven times in a day, and seven times in a day returns to you, saying, 'I repent,' you shall forgive him" (vv. 3-4).

> To repent means "to change one's mind."... Such repentance is essential to Christ's pattern of forgiveness. He makes it clear that those who sin against us must be brought to the place where their failure to love is admitted.[1]

Respected author and counselor Jay Adams adds additional scriptural ammunition to the repentance debate:

> It should go without saying that since our forgiveness is modeled after God's (Ephesians 4:32), it must be conditional. Forgiveness by God rests on clear, unmistakable conditions. The apostles did not merely announce that God had forgiven men.... Paul and the apostles turned away from those who refused to meet the conditions, just as John and Jesus did earlier when the scribes and the Pharisees would not repent.[2]

I will admit that both of these writers offer a compelling case. There are at least three powerful arguments for demanding repentance before granting forgiveness.

"FORGIVENESS NEEDS TO BE EARNED"

When someone injures us (so this argument goes), they have created a cosmic debt that somehow must be satisfied. To offer forgiveness to an unrepentant person is fundamentally unfair.

Think about the story of the prodigal son for a moment. One day he broke his father's heart by demanding his share of the inheritance.

What the boy was really saying to his dad was this: "I know this money will come to me one day when you're gone, but I'm tired of waiting around for you to die, so give it to me now." Without any argument or objection, the father quietly acquiesced to the son's demands and gave him his share of his estate.

As you remember, it took no time at all for the boy to dissipate his inheritance on wine, women, and who knows what else. One day he found himself slopping the pigs (one can hardly think of a more degrading task for a Jewish man) and even coveting their food. At that moment, the Bible says, he "came to his senses." Realizing that even his father's servants had more to eat than he did, he decided to return home.

> And he got up and came to his father. But while he was still a long way off, his father saw him, and felt compassion for him, and ran and embraced him, and kissed him. And the son said to him, "Father, I have sinned against heaven and in your sight; I am no longer worthy to be called your son." But the father said to his slaves, "Quickly bring out the best robe and put it on him, and put a ring on his hand and sandals on his feet; and bring the fattened calf, kill it, and let us eat and be merry; for this son of mine was dead, and has come to life again; he was lost, and has been found." And they began to be merry. (Luke 15:20-24)

The father was more than willing to forgive the son. But before he could welcome the son back into the family (some people claim), he first had to hear the words "Father, I have sinned." Here is more evidence, we're told, that forgiveness must be earned.

The only problem with this argument is that there's always a deficit between what our offender owes us and what, in fact, he is able to pay. In the parable we looked at in the last chapter about the unforgiving slave, there was a tremendous disparity between the slave's debt and the slave's resources. Although the slave begged for mercy and promised to repay everything, the debt was too large for him to erase in a thousand lifetimes, much less one.

The situation would seem less hopeless for the second slave in that story. He owed only sixteen dollars. Surely anyone could scrape together a few dollars to retire a debt, especially if the alternative was going to prison. Yet the slave's paltry assets were insufficient to cover even this relatively small obligation.

The point is that both situations — the first slave's debt to the king and the second slave's debt to the first slave — though different in many respects, still shared one thing in common: Both creditors were holding an account receivable that was basically worthless. Only the king realized this, however, as he decided to absorb the loss himself.

The first slave was not so insightful. He mistakenly thought that imprisoning and torturing his fellow slave would somehow enrich him, or least console him over the forfeited debt. Yet in the end, he collected no more of what was due him than the king did.

Those who demand repentance before granting forgiveness are operating under the illusion that somehow their offender's repentance will be sufficient to cover the offense. The words "I'm sorry" may be powerful enough to bring momentary relief to a wound, but they are insufficient in themselves to effect permanent healing.

Isn't that true in our relationship with God? Is there anything we could ever do to earn God's forgiveness? Is saying "I'm sorry" enough to erase the stain of

an abortion
a divorce
an affair
a broken vow to God

How silly (and prideful) it is to think that we could ever repay our Creator for the hurt we have inflicted upon Him by any act of penitence, much less uttering a simple "I'm sorry." Mark it down, circle it, and remember this forever: We are not saved by our repentance but by God's grace.

> For by *grace* you have been saved through faith; and that not of yourselves, it is the gift of God; not as a result of works, that no one should boast. (Ephesians 2:8-9)

As we'll see in the next chapter, repentance plays a vital role in the forgiveness process, but repentance is powerless in and of itself to secure forgiveness.

"Forgiving an Unrepentant Person Invites Further Abuse"

If a woman forgives her philandering husband before he expresses any remorse, isn't she in effect wearing a "Kick Me" sign? By absolving his sin without at least insisting on a "Please forgive me," aren't we doing a fundamental disservice to both the offender as well as society?

Imagine that your teenager breaks a curfew. You confront him about his failure to abide by the rules of the house, but he expresses no remorse. What do you do? You could say that you forgive him and hope it never happens again. But unless he expresses genuine sorrow for what he's done, aren't you inviting further abuse?

I read of a professor from a Christian university who encountered one of the university's students in Europe and discovered he was having an affair with another woman while his wife was at home in the United States. The professor reminded the student that God would certainly discipline him for his disobedience. The student responded nonchalantly, "I expect God to forgive me — that's His job."

That's why forgiveness can be dangerous business. Grace without repentance — an acknowledgment of wrong and a resolve to change — risks further abuse. No way around it.

The apostle Paul recognized the potential abuse of grace. After stating the truth in Christ that "where sin increased, grace abounded all the more," he asked the penetrating question, "What shall we say then? Are we to continue in sin that grace might increase?" (Romans 5:20; 6:1).

The great preacher Dr. Martin Lloyd-Jones, in commenting on this passage, reminds us of the very real risks associated with forgiveness:

> The true preaching of the gospel of salvation by grace alone always leads to the possibility of this charge being brought against it. There is no better test as to whether a man is really preaching the New Testament gospel of salvation than this, that some people might misunderstand it and misinterpret it to mean that it really amounts to this, that because you are saved by grace alone it does not matter at all what you do; you can go on sinning as much as you like because it will redound all the more to the glory of grace. That is a very good test of gospel

> preaching. If my preaching and presentation of the gospel of salvation does not expose it to that misunderstanding, then it is not the gospel. Let me show you what I mean.
>
> If a man preaches justification by works, no one would ever raise this question. If a man's preaching is, "If you want to be Christians, and if you want to go to heaven, you must stop committing sins, you must take up good works, and if you do so regularly and constantly, and do not fail to keep on at it, you will make yourselves Christians, you will reconcile yourselves to God, and you will go to heaven." Obviously a man who preaches in that strain would never be liable to this misunderstanding. Nobody would say to such a man, "Shall we continue in sin, that grace may abound?", because the man's whole emphasis is just this, that if you go on sinning you are certain to be damned, and only if you stop sinning can you save yourselves. So that misunderstanding could never arise....
>
> I would say to all preachers: if your preaching of salvation has not been misunderstood in that way, then you had better examine your sermons again, and you had better make sure that you really are preaching the salvation that is offered in the New Testament to the ungodly, to the sinner, to those who are dead in trespasses and sins, to those who are enemies of God. There is this kind of dangerous element about the true presentation of the doctrine of salvation.[3]

In fairness to the apostle Paul, we should allow him to answer his own question, "Are we to continue in sin that grace might increase?"

> May it never be! How shall we who died to sin still live in it? (Romans 6:2)

To Paul it was unthinkable that a forgiven person who had been freed from the power of sin would ever voluntarily choose to become a servant of sin again. I love the way Max Lucado illustrates the absurdity of such a decision:

> Most of my life I've been a closet slob. I was slow to see the logic of neatness. Why make up my bed if you are going to sleep in it again tonight? Does it make sense to wash dishes after only one meal? Isn't it easier to leave your clothes on the floor at the foot of the bed so they'll be there when you get up and put them on? Is there anything gained by putting the lid on the toothpaste tube tonight only to remove it again tomorrow?...
>
> Then I got married.
>
> Denalyn was so patient. She said she didn't mind my habits...if I didn't mind sleeping outside. Since I did, I began to change. I enrolled in a twelve-step program for slobs. ("My name is Max, I hate to vacuum.") A physical therapist helped me rediscover the muscles used for hanging shirts and placing toilet paper on the holder. My nose was reintroduced to the fragrance of Pine Sol. By the time Denalyn's parents came to visit, I was a new man. I could go three days without throwing a sock behind the couch.
>
> But then came the moment of truth. Denalyn went

> out of town for a week. Initially I reverted to the old man. I figured I'd be a slob for six days and clean on the seventh. But something strange happened, a curious discomfort. I couldn't relax with dirty dishes in the sink. When I saw an empty potato-chip sack on the floor I — hang on to your hat — bent over and picked it up! I actually put my bath towel back on the rack. What had happened to me?
>
> Simple. I'd been exposed to a higher standard.[4]

Max's experience is the essence of Paul's argument in the remainder of Romans 6. Though the downside of God's forgiveness is that it invites further abuse, the benefit of forgiveness is that it exposes us to a higher way of living, so that, as Paul puts it, "we too might walk in newness of life" (Romans 6:4).

Although receiving forgiveness *should* motivate us to change, it doesn't always work that way. Forgiving an unrepentant person can give license to further abuses.

"Forgiving an Unrepentant Person Is Unscriptural"

The strongest argument for demanding repentance before offering forgiveness is that the Bible requires it — at least at first glance. Let's look at some of the scriptural evidence for repentance as a prerequisite for forgiveness.

First, repentance appears to be a condition for receiving God's forgiveness:

> And they went out and preached that men should repent. (Mark 6:12)

> I tell you, no, but, unless you repent, you will all likewise perish. (Luke 13:3)

> If we confess our sins, He is faithful and righteous to forgive us our sins and to cleanse us from all unrighteousness. (1 John 1:9)

> Now when they heard this, they were pierced to the heart, and said to Peter and the rest of the apostles, "Brethren, what shall we do?" And Peter said to them, "Repent, and let each of you be baptized in the name of Jesus Christ for the forgiveness of your sins; and you shall receive the gift of the Holy Spirit. (Acts 2:37-38)

Not only does repentance seem essential to securing God's forgiveness, it also appears to be a condition in granting forgiveness to others. Again, consider the strong scriptural evidence for that position:

> And if your brother sins, go and reprove him in private; if he listens to you, you have won your brother. But if he does not listen to you, take one or two more with you, so that by the mouth of two or three witnesses every fact may be confirmed. And if he refuses to listen to them, tell it to the church; and if he refuses to listen even to the church, let him be to you as a Gentile and a tax-gatherer. (Matthew 18:15-17)

> Be on your guard! If your brother sins, rebuke him; and if he repents, forgive him. And if he sins against you seven

> times a day, and returns to you seven times, saying, "I repent," forgive him. (Luke 17:3-4)

> Therefore, confess your sins to one another, and pray for one another, so that you may be healed. (James 5:16)

The heart of the argument is really quite simple. If (a) God requires us to acknowledge our sin before He forgives us, and (b) we are to forgive others in the same way God has forgiven us (Ephesians 4:32), then it seems to follow naturally that (c) we should require our offender to repent before we forgive him.

It's a logical conclusion — but one that fails to note an important distinction. There's a difference between *receiving* forgiveness and *granting* forgiveness. The issue of repentance is vitally important to accepting forgiveness, but irrelevant to giving forgiveness. In addressing the subject of repentance, we had first better know to whom we are speaking: the offender or the offended.

Perhaps this illustration will help. Every time I preach on the subject of divorce, I feel like I'm walking through a minefield because of the variety of people in our audience: victims of an unwanted divorce, those who are contemplating divorce, those who have divorced their mates for other than biblical reasons, single adults, and those who would never consider divorce. (Murder? Possibly. Divorce? Never.) As a pastor it's important that I present the whole counsel of God when I am preaching a message on divorce, but in a counseling situation it is important for me to know the specific situation of the other person. My counsel is shaped by my audience.

When a husband informs me that he is contemplating leaving his mate to pursue a more fulfilling relationship, it would be inappropriate for me to give him a copy of my book *Guilt-Free Living* to soothe his inevitable pangs of remorse. Instead I should advise him that God hates divorce and remind him of the sanctity of the marriage relationship.

However, if I'm counseling someone who has already divorced and remarried, my advice would differ. There's little profit in reminding that person of his sin and condemning him to a life of unhappiness. Now that the divorce has taken place, I would talk to that person about receiving God's grace and resolving to build a strong marriage.

Similarly, in discussing the relationship between repentance and forgiveness, we must first determine our audience. Are we speaking to the offender or the offended? If someone says, "I want my mate to forgive me for ______," then the issue of repentance is vitally important. But if the wounded party comes to me and says, "I'm having difficulty forgiving my mate because he shows no remorse," then repentance is much less important.

What is repentance? The Greek word translated as "repent" comes from a root word that means "to change one's mind." Repentance is a change of mind that leads to a change of direction. Perhaps you have had the experience of unknowingly traveling down a one-way street and suddenly noticing that all of the traffic is heading toward you (not to mention that all of the street signs are backwards). You're faced with a choice: You can continue to proceed in the wrong direction and suffer the consequences, or you can acknowledge your mistake, make a U-turn, and start heading in the right direction.

Repentance involves acknowledging your wrong direction, making a U-turn, and beginning to travel in a new direction. And in the following four instances, this repentance is vital.

Repentance Is Essential to Receiving God's Forgiveness

Although God's grace is the *basis* for salvation, repentance is the *channel* through which that grace is received. The New Testament letter of 1 John is directed toward Christians, but it teaches a general principle about God's forgiveness that applies to Christians and non-Christians alike: Repentance is a prerequisite for receiving God's forgiveness.

> If we say that we have no sin, we are deceiving ourselves, and the truth is not in us. If we confess our sins, He is faithful and righteous to forgive us our sins and to cleanse us from all righteousness. (1 John 1:8-9)

We'll discuss further the relationship between repentance and God's forgiveness in chapter 8.

Repentance Is Essential to Reconciliation with Another Person

While God requires me to unconditionally forgive the business partner who cheats me, He does not require that I remain in business with him. I can forgive someone without being reunited with that person. But as we'll see in chapter 6, if we want to build a broken relationship (with other people or with God), repentance is necessary.

Repentance Is Essential to Restoration to a Position

In Matthew 18, Jesus discusses two types of offenses: personal offenses and corporate offenses. In that chapter Peter asks, "Lord, how often shall my brother sin *against me* and I forgive him?" (18:21). As we've seen, Jesus answers Peter's question with the parable about the unforgiving slave, illustrating the unlimited, unilateral, and unconditional nature of forgiveness on the personal level.

But how are we to respond to the sinning church member whose lifestyle is the talk of the community? In Matthew 18:15-20, Jesus discusses a procedure for restoring those who have fallen into sin — a procedure that demands repentance. We'll discuss this relationship between repentance and restoration in the next chapter.

Repentance Is Essential to Relief from Guilt

The other day, the "Change Oil Now" indicator appeared on my car's dashboard. I had a choice about how to deal with that warning. I could have reached into my glove compartment and pushed the "reset" button and the light would immediately go out. That temporary solution would have damaged my car in the long run. Or I could stop at a service station and perform the recommended maintenance to preserve the health of my engine.

In the same way, guilt is an indicator that something in our life is wrong. Unfortunately, some people try to prematurely extinguish their guilt by denial ("I'll pretend the light is not on and keep on living") or rationalization ("There must be some other reason I feel this way, so I'll hit the reset button"). King David tried that approach for about six months after one particular sin, and it was wholly ineffective:

> When I kept silent about my sin, my body wasted away
> Through my groaning all day long.
> For day and night Thy hand was heavy upon me;
> My vitality was drained away as with the fever heat of
> summer.
>
> (Psalm 32:3-4)

Only when David repented of his sin did he experience relief from guilt:

> I acknowledged my sin to Thee,
> And my iniquity I did not hide;
> I said, "I will confess my transgressions to the Lord";
> And Thou didst forgive the guilt of my sin."
> (Psalm 32:5)

In each of the four instances in which repentance is vital—receiving God's forgiveness, reconciliation with other people we have wronged, restoration to a position, and relief from guilt—it is the *offender* for whom the repentance is necessary, not the offended.

Now, let's switch audiences. No longer are we speaking to the one who is seeking forgiveness, but to the one who must choose whether or not to grant forgiveness. Can we honestly release another person of their obligation toward us without first demanding their repentance? Is unconditional and unilateral forgiveness biblical, practical, and healthy?

Remember that forgiveness is not synonymous with reconciliation, restoration, or even releasing a person of consequences that might arise from their wrong. Forgiveness is simply saying, "Although you have wronged me and owe me for what you have done, I release you of your obligation toward me."

I believe that I've presented fairly some strong arguments against such unilateral and unconditional forgiveness. Now allow me to briefly make the case *for* unconditionally forgiving an unrepentant offender.

UNCONDITIONAL FORGIVENESS IS BIBLICAL

As we've seen, there are some instances in which the Bible demands repentance. However, forgiveness — releasing someone of his obligation to us for the wrong committed against us — is an action that takes place solely within our own heart. Consider Jesus' words as He applied the parable of the unforgiving slave:

> So shall my heavenly Father also do to you, if each of you does not forgive his brother *from your heart.* (Matthew 18:35)

In the Hebrew mind, the seat of a person's emotions was not the heart, but the bowels. On the other hand, the heart represented a person's mind. For example, the psalmist wrote, "The fool has said in his *heart,* 'There is no God'" (Psalm 14:1). The writer of Proverbs observed, "For as he thinketh in his *heart,* so is he" (Proverbs 23:7, KJV).

Why this short lecture on Hebrew anatomy? Such an understanding helps us interpret and apply Jesus' words about forgiveness. The command to forgive "from your heart" — or literally "from your mind" — implies that forgiveness is a rational choice I can make independent of what others may or may not do.

Jesus again illustrates the unconditional nature of forgiveness in His instructions about prayer:

> And whenever you stand praying, forgive, if you have anything against anyone; so that your Father also who is in heaven may forgive you your transgressions. But if you do not forgive, neither will your Father who is in heaven forgive your transgressions. (Mark 11:25-26)

Understand the scenario Jesus is describing here. You have set your alarm clock twenty minutes early one morning to spend time alone with God in prayer. As you review your lists of requests, some other thought enters your mind. You remember some hateful words that your mate yelled at you several weeks earlier. Instead of confronting your spouse, you chalked it up to a bad day that he or she was having. You congratulated yourself on letting it pass without allowing the disagreement to erupt into Word War III.

But now as you attempt to talk with your heavenly Father, your mate's words drift back into your consciousness. What should you do? Some would misapply Matthew 5:24 ("first be reconciled to your brother, and then come and present your offering") and say that you should seek restoration with your mate before continuing in prayer.

But Jesus had a more radical idea: "Forgive." Whether your spouse is in the next room or the next state is irrelevant. You have the ability to let go of that offense right there in the privacy of your own bedroom, or wherever you might be.

One other thought: What about Jesus' command in Luke 17:3-4 that seems to imply that repentance is a condition for granting forgiveness? Let's look again at Jesus' words.

> Be on your guard! If your brother sins, rebuke him; and if he repents, forgive him. And if he sins against you seven times a day, and returns to you seven times, saying, "I repent," forgive him.

Jesus is describing how we are to respond to those who repeatedly hurt us and then say, "I'm so sorry. I promise it will NEVER happen again." But it does happen again…and again…and again. Just as God refuses to limit His forgiveness, we are not to limit ours. But let's not put words in Jesus' mouth, as some try to do. The verse does not read, "And if he sins against you seven times a day AND IF AND ONLY IF HE REPENTS, forgive him."

Nowhere in this verse does Jesus advise withholding forgiveness from a person who refuses to repent. Repentance is our offender's responsibility; forgiveness is our responsibility.

UNCONDITIONAL FORGIVENESS IS PRACTICAL

Demanding our offender's repentance, remorse, or rehabilitation can be both uncomfortable and impractical. For example, if repentance is a requirement to granting forgiveness then that means we must confront every person who wrongs us before we can genuinely forgive him. Specifically, that means we must always confront

the boss who speaks sharply to us
the friend who forgets our birthday
the mate who forgets to pick up our clothes at the dry cleaner
the pastor who neglects to visit us in the hospital

Without such a confrontation (some believe), we are doomed to a life filled with bitterness.

But do we really want to spend our entire lives demanding repentance from everyone around us? Aren't we ensuring that people will run for the hills when they see us coming if we're always needing to "talk about a personal matter"? And more importantly, doesn't such a confrontational lifestyle contradict the essence of Christian love, a love that "keeps no record of wrongs" (1 Corinthians 13:5, NIV).

John MacArthur writes,

> The heavy emphasis on forgiveness in Scripture is not meant to make us more confrontational, but quite the opposite. When Scripture calls us to have an attitude of forgiveness, the emphasis is always on long-suffering, patience, benevolence, forbearance, kindness, and mercy — not confrontation.[5]

Demanding repentance from our offender can also be impractical. For example, what if you've lost track of the person who has wronged you? Are you automatically sentenced to a lifetime of bitterness just because he left no forwarding address? If your offender is incapacitated by illness or senility, must you carry her offense the rest of your life?

I often talk with people who have been hurt by a parent or grandparent. They desperately long to hear the words "I'm sorry, please forgive me" so they might begin to heal emotionally. But death has rendered the other person incapable of ever demonstrating remorse for his or her sin.

Unconditional forgiveness provides a way we can let go of the wounds of the past inflicted by those who are incapable of repentance.

UNCONDITIONAL FORGIVENESS IS BENEFICIAL

Probably the best reason to forgive unconditionally is the emotional and spiritual healing it brings into our lives. As one person described it,

> So often when people think about forgiveness they think about what it's going to do for someone else.... What

> they don't realize is that forgiveness is really an act of self-interest. We're doing ourselves a favor because we become free to have a more peaceful life — we free ourselves from being emotional victims of others.[6]

Let me illustrate that statement. Possibly you remember attending on old-fashioned picnic and participating in a three-legged race. One of your legs would be bound to the leg of another person. The spectators would roar with laughter as they watched you and your partner trying to hobble to the finish line. "If only I could be freed from this guy I could make better time," you probably thought. But the rules didn't allow for a solo run — you had to remain tied to your partner and could travel only as fast as he did. For better or worse, you and your partner were bound to one another.

Similarly, when you demand repentance, remorse, or rehabilitation from your offender, you have emotionally bound yourself to him. You can travel no farther than he travels. Your progress is limited by his progress. You are doomed to hobble through life together.

But forgiveness provides a way to cut the emotional cord that binds you to your offender. When you release another person from his offense you are saying, "I no longer wish to be emotionally tied to you. Whether you repent or not is now between you and God. I'm ready to move on with my life, and so I release you of any obligation to me."

God wants us to be free of any weight that distracts us from running the race of life. Remember Hebrews 12:1?

> Therefore, since we have so great a cloud of witnesses surrounding us, let us also lay aside every encumbrance and

> the sin which so easily entangles us, and let us run with endurance the race that is set before us.

Unconditional forgiveness allows us to "lay aside every encumbrance" and live a Christ-honoring life.

Christian counselor and author Chuck Lynch illustrates the benefits of unconditional forgiveness by relating the story of one of his clients, a woman named Amber. As a child, Amber had been molested by her grandfather, who was now dead. After Dr. Lynch explained to her the benefits — and in this case the necessity — of unconditional forgiveness, she wrote this letter to her grandfather.[7]

A Gift for Grandpa

> Dear Grandpa,
>
> I am writing this letter to share with you a few changes that have taken place in my life. But first of all I want to tell you thanks for all that you have done for me. You gave me a lot of special memories. For instance, the times you shaved, whipped up your cream, and painted your face. I was always fascinated by all that cream. Then there were times you would let me put the cream on your face. Sometimes I would put the cream on me, but you would never let me shave it off my face. Then there were the times of washing and waxing your car with you to make it shiny and new looking. Sometimes we would splash and play in the water. I want to thank you for loving me and being my friend when there seemed to be no others.

I also want you to know I am on a spiritual journey, working toward inner healing with the Lord Jesus in my heart. But I am having trouble in the area of the things you did to me when I was a little girl. So, through my struggle to help me move on in my healing, I want to give you a gift, the most special gift I could give to you. That gift, Grandpa, is forgiveness. I want to explain to you what kind of forgiveness it is. My gift of forgiveness to you is for all the violations done against me by you when I was growing up. I will explain.

I want to forgive you and release you for violating me by using my body for your own sexual pleasure.

I want to forgive and release you for prematurely stimulating my sexual feelings, something I never understood before as a child.

I want to forgive you and release you for the mistrust you developed in me, training me not to let anyone be too close to me for fear of being hurt.

I want to forgive and release you for making me feel so ashamed when I did nothing wrong.

I want to forgive and release you for setting me up to falsely blame myself for something I could not control or make stop as a little child.

I want to forgive and release you for the anger you developed inside me towards you.

I want to forgive and release you for the hate and fear of men that you instilled in me, even towards my dad, whom I now love with all my heart....

I want to forgive you and release you for deceiving

and lying to me and threatening me not to tell by saying I deserved it. If I deserved it, why? What had I done? I was an innocent child, confused into believing that what you were doing was allowed. (I didn't understand any other way.)

I want to forgive you and release you for shattering my dreams for a happy marriage with someone to really love me. You changed me from what I really was to someone I didn't know, and I didn't understand what was happening to me. But I have faith that through all of this, with God by my side, there is someone special out there for me who will understand what I have gone through and will love me regardless.

The most important thing I want to forgive you and release you for is the distorted picture of God you gave me. You made me blame Him for the sin which you were committing which was not His fault. As a child I could not understand how a God who loved me, and in the Bible said He was there for me and would protect and guide me, could let something like this happen. Now I know that it was not His fault, and He was there all the time for me. But as a scared little girl, I probably did not listen when He tried to talk to me because I did not believe what He had to say.

Grandpa, now that I have completed this part of the journey and transferred you over to the Lord through forgiveness, I want to make a promise in my heart that I will never bring this up against you again.

It is time to draw this letter to a close and say

> good-bye. Before I do, I want to thank you again for all the good memories you have given me. I will always cherish those times. Now that I feel better about myself and can accept what has happened to me, I can really say I know what it means to love you through the eyes of the Lord.
>
> Amber

Perhaps God has brought to your mind the name of someone who has wounded you deeply and is unaware — or worse, unmoved — by his actions. Maybe this person has been separated from you by distance or even death. Are you tired of living with that hurt from the past? Do you wish to experience the same kind of freedom Amber longed for? Unconditional forgiveness is biblical, practical, beneficial, and most importantly, *possible.*

CHAPTER 5

FORGIVENESS AND CONSEQUENCES

Why forgiven people sometimes must sit in the electric chair

Some years ago Chuck Colson, the convicted Watergate defendant who is now president of Prison Fellowship Ministries, traveled with a group of Christian laymen to the Indiana State Penitentiary. Colson and his twenty companions were able to conduct a worship service for twenty inmates on death row.

At the end of the service, Colson and the other believers were allowed to pray individually with the inmates. As his group was preparing to leave, Colson's attention was drawn to a convicted murderer awaiting execution and the Christian volunteer who had been praying with him. The volunteer, who had come with Colson, was accompanying the prisoner as he returned to his cell. Colson followed.

"We have to go," he said to the volunteer. "The warden is waiting to escort us out of the cellblock."

"Chuck, can't you wait a little while longer?"

"We really need to get going," Colson replied. "I have a very tight schedule. Some of us have other appointments."

"Chuck, please," the volunteer pleaded, "this is very important. You see, I am Judge Thomas Dodge, and I sentenced this man, Henry Lewis, to die. But since he was placed in this prison, he has become a Christian, my brother in the Lord. We just need a few more minutes to forgive each other, and to pray for each other, and to love each other."[1]

On a personal level, the judge was willing to forgive the convict for his crime, for the time and emotional energy the judge was required to exert because of the trial, and for any threats the prisoner might have voiced toward the judge. Although the judge held in his hand an "account receivable" for all of those offenses, he was willing to release the convict of his personal obligation.

But such forgiveness did not erase the consequences of the murderer's crime. While the prisoner was forgiven by God, forgiven on a personal level by the judge, and perhaps even forgiven by the victim's family, justice demanded that the prisoner suffer the consequences for his actions.

One of the greatest barriers to forgiveness is the myth that forgiveness automatically frees our offender from any consequences for his actions. Such a misunderstanding makes many people hesitant to forgive and condemns them to a lifetime of unnecessary bitterness.

For example, consider a wife who divorces her husband because of a series of adulterous escapades. She has three small children at home, and her income is insufficient to provide for their growing needs. Her husband is required to pay child support but has become increasingly tardy in his payments. He comes to her begging for mercy. "I know leaving you was wrong, and I'm sorry for the pain I've caused you and the kids. But these support payments are like a noose around my neck and are preventing me from making the new start I need. If you've really forgiven me, please don't make me keep paying for my mistake. Give me a chance for a fresh beginning." Does forgiveness require the woman to agree to reducing her husband's child-support payments?

Or what about the church treasurer who is caught embezzling funds from the weekly offerings. When confronted by other church leaders, he admits his mistake, publicly confesses his theft to the entire congregation, and makes restitution for the stolen funds. By all outward evidence he is a changed man. He desperately desires to be reinstated in his position as treasurer, but some leaders are reluctant to do so. "How do we know he won't do this again?" But others in the congregation argue that true Christian love means expecting the best, not the worst from others. "If we've really forgiven him, why would we insist that he spend the rest of his life paying for his mistake? True forgiveness releases a person from their obligation."

Or consider a woman who was sexually abused by her uncle. Though he has never asked for her forgiveness, she has chosen — for her own benefit — to unilaterally and unconditionally forgive him. Her aunt suspects that her husband is involved in some type of immorality, though she us unaware of any specifics. She confronts her niece with an observation and a direct question: "I've noticed that you've always been standoffish with Henry. I want to ask you a very personal question: Has he ever offended you in any way?" Should the woman answer her question, knowing that it could lead to the breakup of the marriage and possibly prison, if other instances of abuse are uncovered? Or should she deny any impropriety, reasoning that true forgiveness "keeps no record of wrongs"?

Each of the above situations illustrates the same dilemma: Does forgiveness automatically erase the consequences of sin? Have I truly released a person of any obligation to me when I insist that he be held accountable for his actions?

VENGEANCE VS. JUSTICE

The answer to those questions is found in the important distinction between two words: *vengeance* and *justice.* Vengeance is my desire to see another person suffer for the pain he has caused me. The Bible consistently warns against harboring that kind of thirst in our hearts:

> Do not rejoice when your enemy falls,
> And do not let your heart be glad when he stumbles;
> Lest the LORD see it and be displeased,
> And He turn away His anger from him.
> (Proverbs 24:17-18)

> You have heard that it was said, "An eye for an eye, and a tooth for a tooth." But I say to you, do not resist him who is evil; but whoever slaps you on your right cheek, turn to him the other also. (Matthew 5:38-39)

> Never take your own revenge, beloved, but leave room for the wrath of God, for it is written, "Vengeance is Mine, I will repay," says the Lord. (Romans 12:19)

Is there someone who has committed an offense against you? Don't try to settle the score with that person, God says. And make sure you don't gloat when He evens the score.

King David beautifully illustrates that principle in a story found in the opening chapter of 2 Samuel. Remember that David's predecessor,

Saul, was so jealous of David's successes that he hounded him relentlessly and even tried to kill him. But eventually Saul met his "Waterloo," and rather than facing defeat by the godless Philistines, he fell on his own sword.

A young man, an Amalekite, eager to get in good with the new king, brought David the news of his old adversary's death, certain that this would bring joy to the king and perhaps a cabinet position in the new administration. When David asked for an explanation, the young soldier even embellished the details of Saul's death to give himself a bigger role:

> By chance I happened to be on Mount Gilboa, and behold, Saul was leaning on his spear.... Then he said to me, "Please stand beside me and kill me; for agony has seized me because my life still lingers in me." So I stood beside him and killed him, because I knew that he could not live after he had fallen. And I took the crown which was on his head and the bracelet which was on his arm, and I have brought them here to my lord. (2 Samuel 1:6,9-10)

Place yourself in David's sandals for a moment. Imagine that for years you've been hounded by a bitter rival who has made your life a living hell. He has spread lies about you, threatened you, and caused you more sleepless nights than you care to remember. One day you open up the newspaper and read his obituary. You can hardly believe your good fortune.

No more looking over your shoulder.

No more worrying about the lies he might spread.

No more obstacles in your road to success.

In an instant the dark shroud that has suffocated the joy from your life has been lifted. I don't know about you, but I would be tempted to break out the champagne and caviar!

But not David. Read carefully his unusual reaction to the news of Saul's death:

> Then David took hold of his clothes and tore them, and so also did all the men who were with him. And they mourned and wept and fasted until evening for Saul and his son Jonathan and for the people of the LORD and the house of Israel, because they had fallen by the sword. (2 Samuel 1:11-12)

In spite of Saul's numerous offenses against him, David had refused to seek vengeance. That was God's business, not David's. Do you remember the remarkable story in 1 Samuel 26 when David and his men had cornered Saul and had the opportunity to kill him while he was sleeping? Yet on that occasion David had said to his men,

> "Do not destroy him, for who can stretch out his hand against the LORD's anointed and be without guilt?" David also said, "As the LORD lives, surely the LORD will strike him, or his day will come that he dies, or he will go down into battle and perish." (1 Samuel 26:9-10)

David understood that vengeance was God's responsibility, not his. And when God finally exacted justice for Saul's rebellion, David refused to delight in the king's death.

God says that we, like David, are never to seek vengeance. But there is a difference between vengeance and justice. Unlike vengeance, justice is the payment God or others might demand from someone because of a wrong they have committed against us, against another person or group of people, or against society as a whole. While we are to avoid vengeance, we are to seek justice for those who have been wronged:

> Vindicate the weak and fatherless;
> Do justice to the afflicted and destitute.
> (Psalm 82:3)

> Learn to do good;
> Seek justice,
> Reprove the ruthless;
> Defend the orphan,
> Plead for the widow.
> (Isaiah 1:17)

> And what does the LORD require of you
> But to do justice, to love kindness,
> And to walk humbly with your God?
> (Micah 6:8)

What is the distinction between vengeance and justice? Perhaps the following contrasts will help you understand the difference:

Vengeance is our desire for retribution against our offender; justice is the repayment another person demands from our offender.

Vengeance is striving to settle the debt ourselves; justice is allowing someone else to settle the score.

Vengeance leads to bitterness; justice leads to healing.

God says that I am to surrender my desire for vengeance, but I can never surrender another person's responsibility to seek justice.[2]

Some years ago a leader in a church I served was involved in an immoral relationship. When evidence of her moral failure was presented to me, I was devastated. For several weeks I couldn't sleep at night as I thought about the consequences her sin would have on our congregation. Many new Christians would become disillusioned and fall away from the church. Others would feel that I had mishandled the incident, either by being too strict or too lax. Still others would question my judgment in having placed her in a leadership position to begin with.

My sadness then turned to anger as I thought about her betrayal of my trust as her pastor. For several days I had to battle against the desire for vengeance. I had to resist the urge to rejoice when further evidence of her sin came to my attention. As God brought to mind my own failures and His unconditional forgiveness, I genuinely released this person of any debt she owed me for injuring our church in general and my ministry in particular. I forgave her.

But my forgiveness did not relieve me of the responsibility I had as a pastor to report her offenses to church officials and eventually relieve her of her ministry responsibility. Some of her supporters in the church raised some legitimate questions:

"Doesn't God give people a second chance?"

"Shouldn't we forgive and forget like God did?"

"Doesn't the Bible say, 'Let he who is without sin cast the first stone'?"

"Isn't this an opportunity for our church to demonstrate God's grace to our community?"

Although I was able to release this leader from her personal obligation toward me, I could not release her from the consequences of her actions. The church officials determined that her actions had broken a sacred trust with our congregation and had destroyed her integrity with our church.

God deals with us in the same way. Throughout this book we have seen that we are to forgive one another "just as God in Christ also has forgiven us." When God forgives us, He removes the eternal consequences of our sin — eternal damnation — but not necessarily the temporal consequences of our actions. When we trust in Christ as our Savior, God releases us of our obligation toward Him. He gives up His right to vengeance against us. However, we may still have to suffer the pain of

a lost job
a broken marriage
a severed friendship
a life-threatening illness, such as AIDS

WHY CONSEQUENCES?

If God has really forgiven us, why does He make us suffer the consequences of our sinful actions?

The Bible mentions at least three reasons.

Consequences Promote Order in Society

I read a story recently about Chi Chi Rodriguez, the famous golfer. One day he was driving a lot faster than he should have been. As he approached a yellow light, it turned to red, but Rodriguez kept going without slowing down a bit. His friend traveling with him nearly had a heart attack right there on the spot.

"Chi Chi, what in the world are you doing? You went right through a red light! Don't you stop for red lights?"

The golfer explained, "My brother taught me to drive, and he doesn't stop for red lights. So I don't stop for red lights."

Sure enough, he approached another red light and zoomed right through it. His friend couldn't stand it any longer.

"You're going to get us killed. What in the world are you thinking about?"

Rodriguez said only, "My brother taught me to drive, and he doesn't stop for red lights. So I don't stop for red lights."

Driving a little farther, they approached an intersection with a green light and Rodriguez hit his brakes, stopped the car, and nervously looked both ways.

"Why are you stopping at a *green* light?" the friend wanted to know.

Rodriguez answered, "Because my brother might be coming!"[3]

Think what our world would be like if there were no red lights. Imagine the chaos that would engulf the world if everyone was free to do as he pleased without any consequences. If your boss ticks you off, kill him. If you're running a little short of cash this month, steal some. If the attorney's questions are too personal, lie. If your neighbor's wife excites you, sleep with her.

The whole rationale for the establishment of government was to provide a means to enforce God's code of conduct and save the world from anarchy. For example, prior to the flood, Noah's world was filled with chaos:

> Now the earth was corrupt in the sight of God, and the earth was filled with violence. And God looked on the

> earth, and behold, it was corrupt; for all flesh had corrupted their way upon the earth. (Genesis 6:11-12)

But after the flood, God established a foundation for government to maintain order in the world through a system of laws and penalties. No longer would man be able to murder without experiencing consequences:

> Whoever sheds man's blood,
> By man his blood shall be shed,
> For in the image of God
> He made man.
>
> (Genesis 9:6)

Later in the Old Testament we see God's love for the chosen nation of Israel as He provided a sacrificial system to atone for their sins. Nevertheless, God's forgiveness did not remove the penalties for disobedience. As the children of Israel prepared to enter into the Promised Land, Moses reminded them of the choice before them: Obey God and prosper; disobey God and experience the consequences:

> See, I have set before you today life and prosperity, and death and adversity; in that I command you today to love the LORD your God, to walk in His ways and to keep His commandments and His statutes and His judgments, that you may live and multiply, and that the LORD your God may bless you in the land where you are entering to possess it. But if your heart turns away and you will not

> obey, but are drawn away and worship other gods and serve them, I declare to you today that you shall surely perish. You shall not prolong your days in the land where you are crossing the Jordan to enter and possess it. (Deuteronomy 30:15-18)

God deals with us in the same way today. Although God may occasionally exempt us from experiencing the full consequences of our actions, that is not the norm. God uses consequences to maintain order in our families, in our churches, and in our society. The father who prematurely posts bond for his son who is accused of drunk driving, the church leader who covers over the sin of a church member, and the victim who argues leniency in the sentencing of their offender — all may have wonderful motives. But they are actually tampering with God's method for maintaining order.

Consequences Serve as a Deterrent to Others

Another reason God usually allows us to experience some consequences for our disobedience is that those consequences can be a powerful deterrent to others.

Consider the example of Ananias and his wife, Sapphira. These two members of the early church sold a piece of property and claimed to give all of the proceeds to the church, but they actually kept a portion of the money for themselves. Their sin was not that they kept some of the money, but that they lied about it to the church. Ananias and then his wife were separately confronted about their wrongdoing, and the consequences they suffered had an unmistakable impact upon other people:

> But Peter said, "Ananias, why has Satan filled your heart to lie to the Holy Spirit, and to keep back some of the price of the land?"... And as he heard these words, Ananias fell down and breathed his last; and great fear came upon all who heard of it....
>
> Now there elapsed an interval of about three hours, and his wife came in, not knowing what had happened.... Then Peter said to her, "Why is it that you have agreed together to put the Spirit of the Lord to the test?"... And she fell immediately at his feet, and breathed her last; and the young men came in and found her dead, and they carried her out and buried her beside her husband. And great fear came upon the whole church, and upon all who heard of these things. (Acts 5:3-11)

My friend and mentor Howard Hendricks says that had Peter passed the plate right then, he could have collected the largest offering in the history of the church! Fear of consequences is a powerful incentive for obedience.

That explains why Paul instructed the young pastor Timothy not to cover over the sins of church leaders:

> Those who continue in sin, rebuke in the presence of all, *so that the rest also may be fearful of sinning.* (1 Timothy 5:20)

I realize that the context of this command is the church, but I think it relates to other arenas of life as well. Although your teenage daughter may truly repent of her third speeding ticket, revoking her driving privileges for a period of time might not only deter her, but also a sibling, from engaging in reckless behavior. Terminating an employee for padding his expense account may promote a sudden surge of honesty among other employees as well. Negative consequences can be a deterrent to evil.

Consequences Inoculate Us Against Further Disobedience

In my book *Say Goodbye to Regret,* I tell about a man named Jack who came to me for counseling. He had been involved in an emotional affair with a coworker for several years but had finally broken it off. God used a number of events to get Jack's attention during his years of disobedience, including the loss of his business.

Although the affair was over, Jack was still suffering the effects of a failed business and a broken trust with his wife. "If God has truly forgiven me," he wanted to know, "why do I keep suffering the consequences of my sin?"

I suggested that Jack view these consequences in a different light. "Jack, how likely are you to get involved with another woman?"

"Every time I see another woman I want to run in the opposite direction. I never want to go through that pain again."

"Do you think you would feel that way if you had not had this affair and suffered the consequences?"

"No. I've always been kind of a flirt and had trouble in my moral life."

"So, in a way, this whole experience with your coworker has inoculated you against any future affair?"

"I never thought of it that way, but I guess you're right."

"Then why don't you thank God for that whole experience."

"You mean, thank God for my sin?"

"Not for your sin, but for His allowing you to go through that experience without losing your family and for giving you the ability to turn away from that sin and learn from your mistake. You can even thank God for the failed business and your less-than-perfect marriage, since those consequences have given you a distaste for any future affairs."[4]

God uses consequences to bring us back into a right relationship with Him...and keep us there! We see this practical result in the psalmist's words: "Before I was afflicted I went astray, but now I keep Thy word" (Psalm 119:67).

WALKING THE TIGHTROPE

Admittedly, there is sometimes a thin line between vengeance and justice. The capacity for self-delusion is infinite. I may think I'm seeking justice when in fact I'm thirsting for vengeance. Sometimes our position of responsibility may require that we seek justice for offenses committed against *us*.

For example, my brother, a policeman, was forced to kill a criminal who was shooting at him. The criminal wronged my brother on a personal level, and my brother should forgive him. But such forgiveness should not keep my brother from exercising his responsibility as a law-enforcement officer and returning fire.

Or consider a father who is infuriated by his son's disobedience. Although the dad has been wronged on a personal level and should forgive his son, he also has a responsibility as a parent to discipline his son.

A similar case is an employer who's slandered by an employee. Although the employer should forgive the gossip being spread by his subordinate, as a leader he cannot allow such behavior to undermine office morale and productivity.

Whenever our position dictates that we confront another person who has wronged us, it's important for us to check our motivation. Are we seeking justice or desiring vengeance? That's why it's best, whenever possible, to allow someone else to mete out the consequences for injuries we suffer. If we're wronged by another person, Christ says our response is to "forgive from the heart." If there must be consequences for our offender's actions, then let someone else demand them, if at all possible.

Specifically, the Bible teaches that there are three administrators of justice in our society.

The Government

In Luke 18:1-8, Jesus told a story about a widow being mistreated by her opponents, and so she went to a judge to seek protection. Nowhere does Jesus condemn the woman for appealing to the governing authorities for justice. Why? The apostle Paul tells us in Romans 13:1-4:

> Let every person be in subjection to the governing authorities. For there is no authority except from God, and those which exist are established by God. Therefore he who resists authority has opposed the ordinance of God; and they who have opposed will receive condemnation upon themselves. For rulers are not a cause of fear for good behavior, but for evil.... [F]or it is a minister of

> God to you for good. But if you do what is evil, be afraid; for it does not bear the sword for nothing; for it is a minister of God, an avenger who brings wrath upon the one who practices evil.

The wife who is suffering physical abuse, the adult who is concerned about the welfare of a child, or the citizen concerned about the illegal activity of a neighbor should never be reluctant to appeal to the government for help. Although we can personally forgive the offender if we have suffered loss, we can appeal to the government for justice.

The Church

Many times the offenses we suffer have consequences that impact the body of Christ. A church member who has bilked you out of your life savings has certainly damaged you, but his dishonesty could also harm other Christians and the reputation of Christ. While you might be able to forgive him personally, you're probably not the best person to confront him about his poor Christian testimony.

But *someone* needs to, and Jesus has given Christians a very precise procedure to follow in that situation (see Matthew 18:15-20). We'll discuss the steps to restoration in the next chapter.

God

Occasionally when we have been wronged, God will directly intervene by bringing disastrous judgments against our offender. These judgments may include illness, financial reversal, family disruptions, or even death.

As a result of Korah's relentless attacks upon Moses, God opened up the earth and swallowed Korah and his followers (Numbers 16:31-32).

Moses never had to lift a finger; God took care of the problem all by Himself.

A CLOSING THOUGHT

I realize that throughout this book I've been addressing two different audiences: those who are struggling with granting forgiveness to others and those who are desiring to receive forgiveness.

If you're wrestling with granting forgiveness, I encourage you not to confuse forgiveness with justice. One reason you may find it difficult to forgive is that you're operating under the illusion that your forgiveness will relieve your offender of any consequences for his offense. Remember, you may release your offender from any moral obligation toward you without exempting him from the consequences that you, or preferably others, will pursue.

If you desire to be on the receiving end of forgiveness, don't expect forgiveness to automatically erase the consequences of your action. A nail driven into a board can be removed, but the hole still remains. Consequences are God's way of maintaining order in society, encouraging obedience in others, and discouraging us from further disobedience.

Chuck Swindoll clearly distinguishes between forgiveness and consequences in his book on the life of David:

> Grace means that God, in forgiving you, does not kill you. Grace means that God, in forgiving you, gives you the strength to endure the consequences. Grace frees us so that we can obey our Lord. It does not mean sin's consequences are automatically removed. If I sin and in the process of sinning break my arm, when I find forgiveness from sin, I still have to deal with a broken bone.[5]

If you're struggling to move past the deep wounds inflicted by another person, I encourage you to release your desire for vengeance and allow God or others to pursue justice. Trust me, He can settle the score much more effectively than you!

If you desire forgiveness from God or others, do not become discouraged over the lingering consequences of your sin, but view those consequences as a gift designed to keep you close to the Father who loves you.

Chapter 6

Forgiveness and Reconciliation

"I forgive you, but I don't want to have dinner with you (or breakfast or lunch for that matter)"

Years ago there was a popular afternoon television program called *Queen for a Day* in which some unsuspecting housewife was selected from the audience, adorned with a crown and scepter, and treated royally for the next half-hour. For a few moments I want to invite you to participate in a similar game that we'll call "Pastor for a Day." Unexpectedly, you have been selected from your congregation to sit in your minister's chair. Instead of a crown and scepter, we're going to give you a Bible plus three people who have come to you for counsel.

What advice will you offer in each of their situations?

An Abused Wife

Sally tells you that she and her husband, John, had been high-school sweethearts and married right after graduation. But throughout their eight years of marriage, John has physically abused her.

Recently Sally persuaded John to attend a marriage enrichment seminar offered by her church. John was impressed with what he heard, and when the speaker invited those in the audience who wanted to become a Christian to raise their hands, Sally was thrilled to see her husband respond. However, within several days the physical abuse resumed — as evidenced by the bruises you notice on her arm.

"That night after the seminar," Sally says, "John asked me to forgive him, and I did. But now things are worse than ever, and I'm really afraid. I asked several friends if they thought I should move out, and they said, 'No, if you move out you're giving him a reason to divorce you. If you've really forgiven him, you'll try to keep your marriage together. Trust God to take care of you.'

"What do you think, pastor?" Sally asks. "Should I stay and trust God, or should I leave?"

Does forgiveness demand that Sally remain with her husband? Why or why not?

An Untrusting Church Worker

Frank, the chairman of your church's elders, has invited you to lunch to discuss a matter that has been "troubling" him for a few days. You dread such appointments because they almost always result in a request for you to don your black-and-white referee outfit and make a call that's likely to be criticized either way you go. As Frank begins speaking, you realize you're there again.

"Pastor, as you know, you requested Bill and me to serve on the long-range planning committee. However, I don't believe we'll be able to work together. I haven't told this to anyone, but ten years ago Bill and my son were involved in a business deal, and, well, Bill cheated my son out of twenty-five thousand dollars. Although he never admitted his wrong, our family forgave him and refused to press charges. But I have to tell you, Pastor, I don't trust him and would feel like a hypocrite serving with him. So you need to decide which one of us you want to serve on the committee."

Is Frank's concern legitimate, or is he still harboring bitterness toward Bill? Try and enjoy your lunch.

A Concerned Daughter

It's almost five o'clock, and your last appointment for the day has arrived. Sara is one of your most faithful church members, as is her husband, Steve.

Several years ago, Sara tells you, her father began an affair with his secretary and, to everyone's shock, divorced his wife and married his lover. Since then her father and his new wife have lived in a different state and have had no contact with Sara and Steve and their young daughter.

But last week Sara received the following letter:

> Dear Sara:
>
> I know that there is no way you can understand what happened between your mother and me many years ago. I admit that our problems were not her fault alone. My choice to divorce her and marry Denise may not have been the best choice, but it is the only alternative I thought I had in order to enjoy any measure of happiness the rest of my life.
>
> Here is my request of you. Denise and I are moving back to your city next month and want to build a relationship with you and Steve and little Darla. I am not

> asking you to condone the choices I have made. But please do not deny me the pleasure of seeing my only grandchild. You have said that you forgive me for my mistakes and yet you have resisted all attempts of reconciliation. How can you truly forgive someone and yet refuse to have any contact with him?
>
> I am really in no position to demand anything from you, but I am asking you to search your heart and ask God to reveal to you whether or not you have, in fact, forgiven me. If you have, I believe you will not continue to refuse to allow me to see my granddaughter.
>
> I await your reply,
>
> Dad

These words haunt Sara. She tells you she doesn't believe her father has genuinely repented of his wrongdoing, and she's concerned about exposing her daughter to an adulterous grandfather who is "living in sin."

Is Sara's demand for repentance really a thinly veiled desire for vengeance? If she has truly released her father of his obligation toward her, shouldn't she desire some type of reconciliation with him? How long must her father continue to pay for his mistakes? Isn't there some kind of statute of limitations on adultery?

Another Barrier

In the last several chapters we've been identifying misunderstandings about forgiveness that prevent people from either granting or receiving this all-important gift. Some people are confused about forgiveness and repentance, thinking that their offender must demonstrate remorse for his action (or at least acknowledge it) before forgiveness is granted. Others are hesitant to forgive because they believe forgiveness means releasing their offender of any consequences for his actions.

A third barrier to forgiveness is illustrated in the three counseling situations described above: confusing forgiveness with reconciliation. Maybe you're one of those people who is hesitant to offer forgiveness because you have absolutely no desire to be reunited with

that mate who has cheated on you
that friend who has repeatedly slandered you
that boss who has continually abused you

In this chapter we'll explore the difference between forgiveness and reconciliation. While I can unilaterally forgive another person, I cannot unilaterally be reconciled to my offender. Forgiveness depends upon *me;* reconciliation depends upon *us.*

THE CASE FOR RECONCILIATION

While extolling the virtue of forgiveness, some authors downplay the importance of reconciliation. They say it's vital that you forgive your adulterous mate or incestuous relative, but whether you ever reestablish a relationship with that person is of secondary importance.

Such a cavalier attitude toward reconciliation contradicts the teaching of Scripture. Consider what the Bible says about the importance of unity among Christians:

> Behold, how good and how pleasant it is
> For brothers to dwell together in unity!
> (Psalm 133:1)

> If therefore you are presenting your offering at the altar, and there remember that your brother has something against you, leave your offering there before the altar, and go your way; first be reconciled to your brother, and then come and present your offering. (Matthew 5:23-24)

> Now all these things are from God, who reconciled us to Himself through Christ, and gave us the ministry of reconciliation. (2 Corinthians 5:18)

> ...being diligent to preserve the unity of the Spirit in the bond of peace. There is one body and one Spirit, just as also you were called in one hope of your calling. (Ephesians 4:3-4)

> Make my joy complete by being of the same mind, maintaining the same love, united in spirit, intent on one purpose. (Philippians 2:2)

> And beyond all these things put on love, which is the perfect bond of unity. (Colossians 3:14)

Make no mistake about it: God desires reconciliation among Christians for at least two important reasons.

First, reconciliation testifies of God's power. The corollary to that is that disharmony among believers is a detriment to our witness.

Gifted author Karen Mains vividly describes the consequences of disharmony among believers in a parable she calls "A Brawling Bride." Picture in your mind the climactic moment of a wedding ceremony. The groom stands at the front in a spotless tuxedo, smiling and full of anticipation as he awaits the entrance of his bride. The attendants are all elegantly dressed. Finally, the pipe organ swells to a crescendo and the familiar strains of the wedding march begins. The audience rises and looks toward the door to catch their first glimpse of the bride.

Suddenly there's a gasp from the crowd. Instead of a beautiful woman dressed in white, the bride is limping down the center aisle, her dress ripped and soiled. Her nose is bleeding, and one eye is purple and swollen shut.

"Does not this handsome groom deserve better than this?" Mains asks. "Alas, His bride, the church, has been fighting again."[1]

I'll never forget hearing a Christian judge tell of how embarrassed he was by the number of people from his church who stood in his court seeking a divorce. "It is destroying the witness of our church in this city," he said.

Without reconciliation, we fail to offer the world what Jesus pointed to as the signal evidence of our faith — our ability to live in harmony with other Christians. "By this all men will know that you are My disciples, if you have love for one another" (John 13:35).

The second reason God desires our reconciliation is that it empowers us to resist the attacks of the enemy. One of Satan's primary strategies is to divide, isolate, and conquer his victims. I've seen Satan successfully implement this plan more times than I care to remember. Two Christians become involved in a dispute over a failed marriage, an unsuccessful business venture, or a betrayal in a friendship. One or both parties become disillusioned and fall away from the church and into spiritual isolation. Once they are cut off from the spiritual nourishment and encouragement they receive from a body of believers, they become easy marks for the enemy's final assault.

Reconciliation is important among Christians because there is spiritual strength in numbers. The gifted Bible expositor Martyn Lloyd-Jones wrote about the value of unity as he recalled the bombing attacks on Britain by Hitler's Luftwaffe during World War II:

> How often during the last war were we told of the extraordinary scenes in air-raid shelters; how different people belonging to different classes...in the common need to shelter from the bombs and death, forgot all the differences between them and became one. This was because in the common interest they forgot the divisions and the distinctions.... In periods of crises and common need all distinctions are forgotten and we suddenly become united.[2]

We should never forget that we are in a war — a spiritual war — "not against flesh and blood, but against the rulers, against the powers, against the world forces of this darkness, against the spiritual forces of wickedness in the heavenly places" (Ephesians 6:12). That's why it is vital that we put aside our differences and join forces to battle against our common enemy instead of against one another. Divorces, lawsuits, church splits, and fractured friendships destroy our witness to the outside word and give the enemy an open invitation to destroy us as well.

Nevertheless, while reconciliation between Christians is always *preferable,* it isn't always *possible.* The apostle Paul advised in Romans 12:18, "If possible, *so far as it depends on you,* be at peace with all men."

Although I can immediately, unconditionally, and continually forgive someone who has hurt me, I may not always be able to effect a reconciliation with my offender. Similarly, if I have hurt another person, I can express my desire for reconciliation, but I am in no position to demand it — just as I can ask for his forgiveness, yet not demand it. The offended person, not the offender, holds all the cards.

Husbands are particularly notorious for their lack of understanding of this important principle. Josh had been verbally abusing his wife for years. After one particularly violent argument, Susan finally demanded that he move out of the house, which he did. Josh now recognizes how wrong he has been and has sought help from a Christian counselor. He cannot understand, however, why Susan will not let him move back into their home. The more he demands to return home, the more resistant Susan becomes. The more resistant she becomes, the harsher Josh becomes, and the relationship spirals downward.

I explained to Josh that there are three ingredients necessary to effect a reconciliation with someone we have wronged — repentance, restitution, and rehabilitation. Some, if not all, of these three ingredients may be required before the person we've wronged will choose to resume or rebuild the fractured relationship, even after that person has fully forgiven us.

REPENTANCE

While I can forgive a person who never admits that he has hurt me, I probably can never be reconciled with him. Why? Relationships are built on common ground.

The prophet Amos asked the question, "Can two walk together, except they be agreed?" (Amos 3:3, KJV). Obviously, it's possible to maintain relationships with people who disagree with us on *some* issues.

You may like Mexican food while your mate prefers Italian. Usually a person's political affiliation is not a litmus test for a friendship. In many churches premillenarians and amillenarians coexist peacefully, along with the majority who have no idea what those words mean. Yet, on important issues, there must be common agreement for a relationship to thrive, and there's no more important issue (at least in our minds) than how another person treats us. If we feel we've been severely wronged, and the other party maintains his innocence, then there's a rupture in the relationship.

That truth applies also to our relationship with God. Failure to acknowledge our sin, even as Christians, breaks our relationship with our heavenly Father. In fact, it's that very relationship Amos had in mind when he wrote, "Can two walk together, except they be agreed?" The prophet was asking the Israelites a rhetorical question: How can you expect God's blessings when you won't admit your sin? Confession of our sin is necessary to maintain our relationship with God.

Admittedly, this is a controversial issue in many circles. Some Christian teachers maintain that confession of sin for a Christian is redundant and unnecessary. "If Jesus Christ forgave you of all of your sins when you trusted in Him, why do you need to ask forgiveness again?"

Good question, but one that fails to differentiate between what one writer terms "judicial" and "parental" forgiveness. When we place our faith in Jesus Christ for our salvation, we're declared "not guilty" by God the Father. In chapter 2 we examined how God accomplished that declaration through the act of imputation. Judicially (legally), God has forgiven us. We are His children, and nothing we do will ever change that relationship.

But that forgiveness does not exempt us from experiencing God's parental disapproval for our sin. For example, when one of my daughters disobeys me, I don't disinherit her and throw her out of the house to fend for herself. She will always be my child, regardless of her behavior. However, there will be a disruption in our relationship as long as she is unwilling to admit her wrong. I'm forced to discipline her, and for a period of time that discipline may drive her away from me. Only when she's willing to admit her mistake and ask my forgiveness will there be a reconciliation in our relationship.

The apostle John had that parental type of forgiveness in mind when he penned these words:

> If we say that we have no sin, we are deceiving ourselves, and the truth is not in us. If we confess our sins, He is faithful and righteous to forgive us our sins and to cleanse us from all unrighteousness. If we say that we have not sinned, we make Him a liar, and His word is not in us. (1 John 1:8-10)

John is saying that as long as a Christian (remember, 1 John was written to believers, not unbelievers) refuses to admit his sin, he is calling God a liar. Can you see how such an accusation might result in God's disapproval and discipline? Confession — agreeing with God about our sin — is necessary for reconciliation with Him.

The same truth applies in our relationship with other people. We must be willing to admit our mistakes and acknowledge the pain we have caused another person before we can ever hope for reconciliation. Why?

Imagine the following scenario. For twenty years Kent has always sent Alicia flowers on their anniversary. This year things were hectic at the office, and Kent has forgotten. When he arrives home, Alicia is upset and asks Kent why he neglected such an important date. Although Alicia is not going to divorce her husband over this slight, there's a definite barrier between them.

Kent has several options. He can protest his innocence by insisting, "I didn't forget. I ordered some flowers today but the florist must have sent them to the wrong address." He would be choosing to be dishonest with his wife. And if she should happen to check with the florist...well, let's just say it could be a chilly anniversary evening.

Or perhaps even worse, Kent might say flippantly, "I'm sorry, but things got so crazy at the office today that our anniversary slipped my mind. I'll try and make it up to you." Although he has offered an apology, he has not expressed regret for the pain he has caused Alicia. In effect, Kent has said, "I may have messed up, but this is really no big deal. Get over it." Not until Kent is willing to admit his mistake and acknowledge the legitimacy of Alicia's pain can he ever hope for a reconciliation.

Obviously, such slights — which occur almost daily — are not the grounds for a legal divorce, but they do create a relational chasm that can be bridged only by repentance. We'll explore later how to express that repentance.

RESTITUTION

Before I choose to rebuild a broken relationship with someone who has wronged me, I may desire to see my offender offer some kind of restitution or payment for his offense. Obviously we need to be careful here not to confuse revenge with restitution. Revenge is the desire to see my offender suffer for the pain he has inflicted on me. As we saw in an earlier chapter, revenge is usually futile because it can never adequately compensate us for the hurt we have suffered. The parent whose child is murdered may desire to see the killer suffer a slow, painful death, but that will never bring his child back to life. Revenge is best left in the hands of God.

However, restitution is our attempt to demonstrate genuine repentance to someone we have wronged. While revenge is the payment we demand from our offender, restitution is the payment we volunteer to another person we have offended.

Some years ago, a church member cheated me out of a rather large amount of money. He had been a trusted friend and his betrayal was painful. However, after a period of time I was able to forgive him for his actions. I surrendered my desire to see him suffer for his sin — but I still wanted my money back! On several occasions he attempted to apologize for his actions, but he never repaid the money, though he had the ability to do so. In my mind, my friend's refusal to make restitution for his actions invalidated his repentance.

The relationship between genuine repentance and restitution is illustrated in the familiar story of Jesus and Zaccheus, the tax collector who was despised by the Jews. In Jesus' day, tax collectors were notoriously dishonest. They were authorized by the Romans to assess taxes, but they were free to inflate the amounts due and to pocket the difference. Imagine having a local IRS agent demand ten thousand dollars from you and learning later that he sent only two thousand dollars to Washington, D.C., and used the rest to buy a new fishing boat. Such practices were legal in the Roman Empire and explain why the Israelites lumped tax collectors together with sinners and Gentiles.

But in spite of his great wealth, Zaccheus was spiritually bankrupt. Fortunately he recognized it and experienced an insatiable hunger in his heart. When he heard that Jesus was coming to Jericho, he was willing to do whatever was necessary to catch a glimpse of the Savior. Let's allow Luke to tell the rest of the story:

> And he was trying to see who Jesus was, and he was unable because of the crowd, for he was small in stature. And he ran on ahead and climbed up into a sycamore tree in order to see Him, for He was about to pass through that way. And when Jesus came to the place, He looked up and said to him, "Zaccheus, hurry and come down, for today I must stay at your house." And he hurried and came down, and received Him gladly. (Luke 19:3-6)

Luke does not tell us all that went on in Zaccheus's home that day. We don't know what the Lord said to him, but apparently Zaccheus embraced Jesus' message as evidenced by this response:

> And Zaccheus stopped and said to the Lord, "Behold, Lord, half of my possessions I will give to the poor, and if I have defrauded anyone of anything, I will give back four times as much." And Jesus said to him, "Today salvation has come to this house." (Luke 19:8-9)

Obviously, Zaccheus's gift to the poor could never atone for his sin against God. Likewise, his willingness to compensate his victims fourfold was generous, but it was incapable of erasing the simple fact that he had wronged them. Nevertheless, Zaccheus's restitution was evidence of the sincerity of his repentance and desire for reconciliation both with God and his fellow Jews.

Imagine for a moment that you were one of Zaccheus's victims. He has extorted ten thousand dollars from you through an inflated tax bill. Because of his dishonesty, your children will have to forfeit going to college next year. Yet as a follower of Christ, you have forgiven Zaccheus of his sin. You have no desire for revenge, but neither do you have any desire for a relationship with this guy. As far as you are concerned, he's history.

One day your best friend says, "Did you hear the news? Zaccheus has become a Christian. I was thinking, I'm sure he could use some Christian friends at this point in his life. Why don't we invite him to be a part of our supper club?"

Although you're genuinely glad to hear of Zaccheus's conversion, you have no desire to associate with this cheat. You're trying to think of a graceful way to blackball your friend's suggestion, when he adds, "And, by the way, did you hear that Zaccheus is going to pay anyone he has cheated four times the amount of money he owes them?" Your attitude would likely change at that moment. Why? Because restitution validates the sincerity of repentance.

REHABILITATION

Another requirement for reconciliation is the rehabilitation of our offender. Before we choose to reestablish a relationship with someone who has wronged us, we may want some assurance that our offender has truly changed so that we aren't victimized once again. It is one thing for someone to be sorry for his actions; it's quite another to be sorry enough to change. The Bible teaches that genuine repentance is evidenced by a change in behavior.

Many people confuse genuine repentance with sorrow. I've counseled abused wives who consider returning to their mates because their husbands are so grief-stricken over the separation. Without trying to appear too cynical, I usually question the sincerity of the husband's remorse. "Do you think that possibly the main reason your husband is so upset is because he no longer has someone to cook his meals, wash his clothes, or sleep in his bed?"

We can be sorry for the consequences of our sin without ever repenting. The apostle Paul contrasted sorrow with repentance in 2 Corinthians 7:10:

> For the sorrow that is according to the will of God produces a repentance without regret, leading to salvation; but the sorrow of the world produces death.

Paul is saying that there is one kind of sorrow that leads nowhere except to a pity party for one. But a godly sorrow leads to definite change in our life. The word "repent" comes from the Greek word *metanoeo* meaning "to change one's mind." Repentance is a change of mind that leads to a change of direction. This word pictures a person who realizes he is headed in the wrong direction, performs a U-turn, and begins heading in a new direction.

Before we rebuild a relationship with an adulterous mate, an incestuous relative, a dishonest employee, or a slanderous friend, we'll probably want some evidence that our offender not only is sorry for his actions, but has made some definite changes in his behavior.

REBUILDING OF TRUST

The kind of rehabilitation necessary for reconciliation doesn't happen instantaneously, and it rarely takes place in a vacuum. Healing a broken relationship takes time, and it usually requires the spiritual assistance of other people.

In Galatians 6, Paul teaches this about restoration:

> Brethren, even if a man is caught in any trespass, you who are spiritual, restore such a one in a spirit of

> gentleness; each one looking to yourself, lest you too be tempted. (Galatians 6:1)

The word translated "restore" is a Greek word used for setting a broken bone. For a bone to properly heal it needs to be placed in a protective cast and given time to properly mend. In the same way, when a person engages in behavior that destroys trust in a relationship, he needs to be surrounded by the spiritual help of other Christians, and he needs time to heal properly. That's why offenders are wrong to demand immediate reconciliation, and why the offended are unwise to offer it. Proper healing in a relationship takes time. A marriage that is fractured through a few moments of adulterous pleasure may take years to rebuild.

What's the difference between forgiveness and reconciliation? Lewis Smedes observes:

> It takes one person to forgive.
> It takes two to be reunited.
> Forgiving happens inside the wounded person.
> Reunion happens in a relationship between people.
> We can forgive a person who never says he is sorry.
> We cannot be truly reunited unless he is honestly sorry.
> We can forgive even if we do not trust the person who wronged us once not to wrong us again.
> Reunion can happen only if we can trust the person who wronged us once not to wrong us again.
> Forgiving has no strings attached.
> Reunion has several strings attached.[3]

CHAPTER 7

FORGIVENESS AND FORGETTING

Why forgetting pain is neither possible nor profitable

Former President Dwight Eisenhower once described his unique method for "forgiving" those who had wronged him:

> I make it my practice to avoid hating anyone. If someone has been guilty of despicable actions, especially towards me, I try to forget him. I used to follow a practice — somewhat contrived I admit — to write the man's name on a scrap of paper, drop it into my bottom drawer and say to myself, "That finishes the incident, and as far as I'm concerned, that person." That drawer over the years became a sort of private wastebasket for crumpled up spite and discarded personalities. Besides, it seemed to be effective and helped me avoid harboring useless black feelings.[1]

Eisenhower may have been a wonderful president, but he did not understand the first thing about forgiveness. Whether or not the former president successfully forgot his offenders, he certainly never forgave them. Forgetting is neither the *means* nor the *test* of genuine forgiveness.

Like Eisenhower, many people confuse forgiveness with forgetting, resulting in two equally disastrous consequences.

First, equating forgetting with forgiveness can short-circuit the forgiveness process. Imagine that you notice an unusual growth on your arm. You know you should go to the doctor to have it checked out, but you're terrified at what the physician might discover, so you do nothing. Over the next few months you have this nagging sensation that something's wrong, but still you refuse to see a physician. You console yourself by talking to friends who reassure you with stories about similar experiences in which the growth was benign.

Finally, the pain in your arm becomes so unbearable that you visit your doctor. He calls a few days later with the results of the biopsy. "I'm sorry but the growth is malignant and has metastasized to other parts of your body. If only we had acted earlier, we might have been able save you."

Likewise, attempting to simply forget our sins or the sins of others against us may provide temporary relief, but not lasting healing. Offenses require the surgical procedure of forgiveness, or else they'll metastasize into bitterness. That's why the writer of Hebrews commands:

> See to it that no one comes short of the grace of God;
> that no root of bitterness springing up causes trouble, and
> by it many be defiled. (Hebrews 12:15)

A second negative outcome that can arise from confusing forgetting with forgiveness is unnecessary guilt. It surfaces in questions like these:

"If God has really forgiven me, why do I keep remembering the affair I had five years ago? Maybe I haven't genuinely repented of my sin."

"If I've really forgiven my father, why can't I forget the hurtful words he spoke to me decades ago? Maybe I haven't really forgiven him."

We looked earlier at some basic misunderstandings such as confusing forgiveness with repentance, with consequences, or with reconciliation. Now we'll look at how forgiveness gets confused with forgetting. While forgetting an offense may be a *result* of forgiveness, it is neither the *means* nor the *test* of genuine forgiveness.

HOLY AMNESIA

Throughout this book we've said that God's forgiveness of us is the model for our forgiveness of others — we're to forgive one another just as God in Christ has forgiven us (Ephesians 4:32, Colossians 3:13). Doesn't the Bible teach that when God forgives, He forgets? If the all-knowing God can bring Himself to forget the grievous sins we've committed against Him, why should we find it so difficult to forget our relatively petty injuries from others?

Since confession is good for the soul, I'll admit that I've used those very clichés myself in some past sermons that hopefully *will* be forgotten.

Let's closely examine the presupposition behind this argument. When God forgives, does He actually forget our sins? On the surface, the Bible seems to teach that He does. Consider the following passages:

> As far as the east is from the west,
> So far has He removed our transgressions from us.
> (Psalm 103:12)

> For I will forgive their iniquity, and their sin I will remember no more. (Jeremiah 31:34)

> He will again have compassion on us;
> He will tread our iniquities underfoot.
> Yes, Thou wilt cast all their sins
> Into the depths of the sea.
> (Micah 7:19)

A casual reading of these verses might lead us to believe that God is capable of completely forgetting our sins when He forgives us. But is it really possible for an omniscient God to suddenly develop a case of heavenly Alzheimer's and completely forget what His creatures have done?

If God has completely forgotten our sins, how can Christians ever have their lives evaluated at the judgment seat of Christ? In 2 Corinthians 5:10, Paul declares,

> For we must all appear before the judgment seat of Christ, that each one may be recompensed for his deeds in the body, according to what he has done, whether good or bad.

If, after we become a Christian, God simply forgets all of our sins — past, present, and future — then it stands to reason that at the judgment seat of Christ, only the good things we've done will come to light. But the Bible says God will examine *all* our deeds: the good, the bad, and the ugly. This is not a judgment to determine our eternal destiny, but our eternal rewards. Nevertheless, those rewards will be tied to our obedience or disobedience in this life, meaning that God must retain some memory of our actions.

"So, Robert, are you saying that you don't believe the Bible when it says that 'God forgets our sins'?" Before you write me off as a heretic, allow me to offer another way of understanding these verses. Although every word in the Bible is God-breathed, not every word is to be taken literally. For example, the Bible refers to God's eyes (2 Chronicles 16:9), His ears (1 Peter 3:12), His hands (Exodus 24:11), His heart (Hosea 11:8), and His feet (2 Samuel 22:10). Yet we know that God is spirit and therefore possesses no physical body. Nevertheless, He does see our actions, hear our prayers, and feel our pain. Those verses are what theologians call "anthropomorphisms" — attempts to explain an infinite God to finite man. The writers of Scripture use the familiar to explain the unfamiliar, much as a teacher might use the dropping of an apple to the ground to explain the law of gravity.

The verses in the Bible that speak of God's forgetting sin are attempts to express the completeness of God's judicial forgiveness of our sin. When we receive God's forgiveness, we no longer have to fear the eternal consequences of our sin. I like what one person said about God's forgiveness: "He casts our sin into the depths of the sea...and then posts a sign that says 'No Fishing.'" Christians never have to worry that one day God will dredge up our sins and say, "I know I forgave you, but the more I think about what you did, I can't allow you into heaven. Adios." No, God has eternally removed the eternal consequences of our sins.

But such forgiveness does not necessitate God forgetting our actions. Romans 4:7-8 (which quotes Psalm 32:1-2) has helped me understand God's forgiveness more completely:

> Blessed are those whose lawless deeds have been forgiven,
> And whose sins have been covered.
> Blessed is the man whose sin the LORD will not take into account.

Did you catch that last phrase? "Whose sin the Lord *will not take into account.*" Our sin creates an indebtedness to God. We owe God for the transgressions we have committed. But Christ's death paid our sin debt in a transaction that Paul explains in Colossians 2:13-14:

> ...having forgiven us all our transgressions, having canceled out the certificate of debt consisting of decrees against us and which was hostile to us; and He has taken it out of the way, having nailed it to the cross.

When you become a Christian, God takes the debt you owe Him, nails it to the cross, and declares it "paid in full." But it is possible to *forgive* a debt without *forgetting* a debt.

Several weeks ago my wife and I decided to give one of our cars to our church. The only problem was that I had misplaced the title. So I had to write the lending institution requesting an official document proving that we had repaid the debt and actually owned the vehicle. Suppose for a moment that I received the following letter back from the lending institution:

> Dear Dr. Jeffress:
>
> Thank you for your letter of March 1. However, we have a policy of destroying records of all of our loans once they are paid in full. Therefore, we are unable to

> provide you with an official release from your debt since we do not know whether such a debt ever existed.
>
> Sincerely,
> General Motors Acceptance Corporation

But the computers at General Motors have long memories. The details of every transaction are forever etched in their memory chips. Let's imagine for a moment that instead of the above letter, I received one that said,

> Dear Dr. Jeffress:
>
> We do indeed have a record of our loan to you and your payment. However, upon further review of this loan, we feel that we let you off too easily. The interest rate we agreed upon was unreasonably low, given market conditions at the time. Therefore, before we can provide you with a release, you must send us an additional $400.
>
> Regretfully,
> General Motors Acceptance Corporation

In this example, General Motors has remembered my debt, but has refused to release me from it. They have taken my debt "into account."

I was grateful that I received no such letter. Instead, the institution sent me a copy of the original loan document detailing the amount of money I had borrowed, the terms of the loan, the interest rate, and — most importantly — the word PAID stamped across it. The institution had forgiven my debt, but they had not forgotten it.

In the same way, God will always remember our sin that required the blood payment of His own Son. But just because God recalls our sin does not mean that He reneges on his promise to forgive our sins. Instead, when Satan brings our sins to God's attention (and passages such as Job 1 and Revelation 12:10 indicate that he does just that!), God doesn't claim a case of holy amnesia. Instead, He reminds our accuser of the death of His Son that has secured our forgiveness. Perhaps that's what the apostle John had in mind when he wrote, "And if anyone sins, we have an Advocate with the Father, Jesus Christ the righteous" (1 John 2:1).

FORGIVENESS VS. MEMORIES

I've counseled a number of people through the years who have struggled with this issue of forgetting their sins. I think about one woman who'd had a prolonged affair with another man, then tried every technique imaginable to erase the memory of those years from her mind. But without any warning, scenes from that illicit relationship would flash across her mind at the most inopportune times: in church, while she was reading her Bible, and even while she was experiencing intimacy with her husband. Her question to me was simple: "If my repentance is genuine and God's forgiveness is complete, why do I still remember those experiences?"

I explained to her one important difference between forgetting and forgiving. Forgetting is a function of the brain; forgiveness is a function of the spirit. In his book *I Should Forgive But...*, Chuck Lynch explains the power of memories this way:

> All memories are stored in the brain by electronic impulses and by chemical transference. Messages are sent simultaneously from nerve to nerve both electronically and chemically. Memory is not a spiritual function — it's

> a biological function. Our brain can store at least six hundred memories a second. That would work out to about one-and-a-half trillion bits of information if we were to live seventy-five years. That is awesome when I consider that I don't even remember what I had for breakfast two days ago.[2]

Although we may not be able to recall certain events in our life, those experiences are nevertheless permanently recorded in our memory banks and could resurface at any time. Thus, when we encourage someone to "forget" an event, we're asking them to do the impossible. In fact, struggling to forget a past event can have just the opposite effect. In *Seventy Times Seven,* David Augsburger explains it this way:

> Just as the man with insomnia, attempting to stop the mad race of his mind, finds that the more he tries to silence his thoughts, the swifter they fly, so the person who struggles blindly to forget only sears the thought more deeply into his memory.[3]

BENEFITS OF REMEMBERING

Here's the bottom line: Forgetting offenses is not *possible*...and neither is it *profitable.* Since God has wired our bodies to permanently record our experiences, there must be positive benefits to remembering our sins.

Consider the experience of the apostle Paul. Before his conversion he was a persecutor of Christians and a blasphemer of God. As much as he may have wanted to, Paul could never escape the daily reminders of his past. His enemies continually voiced their doubts about the legitimacy of his calling. "How could God ever use someone like that?" they wondered. As he went from church to church, he looked into the faces of those whom he had persecuted and the relatives of those he may have killed. Forget his past? Impossible.

But Paul was convinced that there were lasting benefits to remembering his mistakes:

> I thank Christ Jesus our Lord, who has strengthened me, because He considered me faithful, putting me into service; even though I was formerly a blasphemer and a persecutor and a violent aggressor. And yet I was shown mercy, because I acted ignorantly in unbelief; and the grace of our Lord was more than abundant, with the faith and love which are found in Christ Jesus. It is a trustworthy statement, deserving full acceptance, that Christ Jesus came into the world to save sinners, among whom I am foremost of all. And yet for this reason I found mercy, in order that in me as the foremost, Jesus Christ might demonstrate His perfect patience, as an example for those who would believe in Him for eternal life. (1 Timothy 1:12-16)

Although Paul was convinced of God's forgiveness, he never forgot his sin. In fact, the apostle explains three specific benefits of recalling our sin. Remembering our past failures:

Encourages gratitude. "I thank Christ Jesus our Lord," Paul writes. More than thirty years had passed since his conversion, and yet he was still overwhelmed by God's gracious act of forgiveness. Are you? One reason God allows us to remember our sin is so that we might continually recall His undeserved grace.

Extinguishes pride. "Christ Jesus came into the world to save sinners, among whom I am the foremost of all." On God's sin scale, pride ranks right at the top. "God is opposed to the proud, but gives grace to the humble" (1 Peter 5:5). One way God encourages humility is by allowing us to recall our mistakes.

Exhibits grace. "And yet," Paul continues, "for this reason I found mercy, in order that in me as the foremost, Jesus Christ might demonstrate His perfect patience, as an example." Paul understood that his past sins made him Exhibit A of God's ability to forgive. To those who struggled with the possibility of God's forgiveness, Paul said, "Look at me. If God is capable of forgiving *me,* he can certainly forgive you." Nearly two thousand years later, the record of Paul's blasphemous and murderous acts still encourages those who struggle with the issue of grace.

When Memories Won't Go Away

But what about the wrongs others commit against us? If it's impossible to forget the memories of those past offenses, is there a way to effectively handle them?

Over the years I've suggested the following steps for dealing with the memories of other people's offenses.

1. Release them if possible. While it's true that every experience is electronically and chemically stored in our body, some of the trivial hurts of life can be dismissed from our consciousness. Recently a church member apologized to me for a comment she had made several months ago after a service. I wanted to be gracious to her, but I honestly couldn't recall what she had said to me, either because I had been preoccupied at the time or chose not to take her comment seriously. For whatever reason, I had made the decision to dismiss her comment instead of nurturing it into a full-grown offense.

I'm not always that forgiving, I can assure you (or better yet, ask my wife). However, overlooking the trivial hurts of life benefits us as much as it benefits our offender. Remember Proverbs 19:11? "A man's discretion makes him slow to anger, and it is his glory to overlook a transgression."

2. Recall your own failures. Admittedly, some memories of past wrongs cannot be easily dismissed and will require action. In a former church in which I served, a leader was caught in an adulterous relationship but ultimately repented of his sin. Another church member said to me, "I forgive him, but every time I see him I can't help but think about what he did." I appreciated his honesty and offered this suggestion. "The next time you see John, think about one secret sin in your past that you hope no one ever discovers. Picture in your mind what it would be like to have that sin announced — or better yet — displayed on a video screen in front of the entire congregation. Then, thank God for His forgiveness."

Jesus sounded a sobering warning to those who engage in self-righteous condemnation of others without honestly evaluating their own lives:

> Do not judge lest you be judged. For in the way you judge, you will be judged; and by your standard of measure, it will be measured to you. And why do you look at the speck that is in your brother's eye, but do not notice the log that is in your own eye? (Matthew 7:1-3)

3. Remember your past act of forgiveness. The best remedy for painful memories is not forgetting the offense, but remembering your decision to forgive. If you're going to remember a wrong, make sure you *also* remember how you dealt with that wrong.

In writing on this topic, Chuck Lynch asks us to recall the Saturday-morning westerns on television in which the good guy always carried two guns, one on each hip. Whenever the hero was in a shootout, he would draw both guns simultaneously, with lightning speed.

Now imagine you encounter someone who has wronged you in the past. You're equipped with two guns. The gun on the left represents the memory of what that person did to you; the gun on the right represents your act of forgiveness. The key is to draw both guns simultaneously. You don't draw on the memory of the sin without also drawing your act of forgiveness.[4]

Paul illustrates this principle in 1 Corinthians 6:9-10:

> Or do you not know that the unrighteous shall not inherit the kingdom of God? Do not be deceived; neither fornicators, nor idolaters, nor adulterers, nor effeminate, nor homosexuals, nor thieves, nor the covetous, nor drunkards, nor revilers, nor swindlers, shall inherit the kingdom of God.

Some people rip these verses out of context, insisting that anyone who has committed any of these sins cannot go to heaven. But consider this: Aren't we all guilty of at least some of these sins? Who hasn't desired what someone else possesses? Covetous people will not go to heaven, Paul insists. Who hasn't lusted in his heart for another person?

Didn't Jesus equate lust with adultery? But Paul's next comment puts this verse into perspective:

> *And such were some of you;* but you were washed, but you were sanctified, but you were justified in the name of the Lord Jesus Christ, and in the Spirit of our God. (6:11)

Paul reminded the Corinthians of their guilt while in the same breath he recalled their forgiveness.

4. Realize that healing memories takes time. I like the story about the group of workers striking against their company because of low wages. They marched in front of the company gates carrying placards that read: "Time Heals. Time and a Half Heals More!"

Obviously, the passing of time in and of itself cannot heal the wound of a serious offense. It's like your doctor telling you that you have a malignancy in your body, then adding, "Don't worry about it. Time heals all things." Certainly healing can come with the passing of time, but only after the proper surgery and treatment.

In the same way time can diminish the sting of past memories if we've properly forgiven another person. Corrie Ten Boom illustrates this truth with a story from her past. She had been unable to forget an atrocity committed against her while she had served as a prisoner. Although she had forgiven her offender, thinking about the injustice she had suffered was robbing her of sleep years after the event. She asked God to reveal to her why she couldn't forget the hurt she had experienced.

"His help came in the form of a kindly Lutheran pastor," Corrie later wrote, "to whom I confessed my failure after two sleepless weeks. 'Up in that church tower,' the pastor said, nodding out the window, 'is a bell which is rung by pulling on a rope. But you know what? After the sexton lets go of the rope, the bell keeps on swinging. First ding, then dong. Slower and slower until there's a final dong and it stops. I believe the same thing is true of forgiveness. When we forgive, we take our hand off the rope. But if we've been tugging at our grievances for a long time, we mustn't be surprised if the old angry thoughts keep coming for a while. They're just the ding-dongs of the old bell slowing down.'

"And so it proved to be," Corrie said. "There were a few more midnight reverberations, a couple of dings when the subject came up in my conversations. But the force — which was my willingness in the matter — had gone out of them. They came less and less often and at last stopped altogether. And so I discovered another secret of forgiveness: we can trust God not only above our emotions, but also above our thoughts."[5]

The "dongs" that continue to sound in your mind from grievances long past may or may not completely stop, but they can diminish in frequency and intensity. How? By making sure you have let go of the rope through the act of forgiveness.

Part Three

Practicing Forgiveness

CHAPTER 8

RECEIVING THE GIFT

You can't give away what you don't possess

I've been counseling with a man for the last several months who became involved in an affair with a married coworker. This illicit relationship has cost him his marriage, his children, his job, and his reputation. Last night he lamented, "I would give anything if I could rewind the last six months of my life and start over. But that's impossible."

Have you ever felt that way before? If only you could

take back a word spoken in anger
say "no" to that unwise suggestion
say "yes" to a forfeited opportunity
salvage a broken relationship

Unfortunately there's no rewind button in life. However, God does offer us a powerful antidote to heal the regrets of past mistakes. It's called forgiveness.

Up to this point, we've discussed the subject of forgiveness in theory by defining forgiveness and exposing four misconceptions that sometimes prevent us from experiencing it. Now we're ready to actually practice forgiveness by learning how to receive it and how to give it to others.

Throughout this book we've seen that it's impossible to give away something you haven't received. That's why before we can ever hope to grant forgiveness to others, we must first receive forgiveness in our own lives: first from God and then from others.

RECEIVING GOD'S FORGIVENESS

Guilt is one of the most debilitating of all human emotions. It wreaks destruction in our relationships with others and in our relationship with God. Certainly some of the guilt pangs we feel are illegitimate. I hesitate to use the term "false guilt" because this kind of guilt is very *real,* although it's often unnecessary. Even our Christian culture can push unreasonable expectations that, if not met, tend to overwhelm us with guilt. For example:

Women should not work outside the home.

We must pray at least an hour a day to have an effective prayer life (preferably before the sun rises).

We should never go into debt.

The only way to properly educate our children is by sending them to a Christian school (or better yet, home school).

But illegitimate guilt isn't nearly the problem some would have you believe that it is. As I mentioned earlier, the main reason people feel guilty is that they *are* guilty. All of us have certain things in our life of which we're ashamed. The story is told of a prominent playwright in London who sent the following anonymous note as a joke to twenty of London's leading citizens: "All has been found out. Leave town at once." All twenty citizens immediately left the city.

Unresolved guilt affects us both emotionally and spiritually. One psychiatrist estimated that 70 percent of people in mental wards could be released today if they knew how to find forgiveness.

Guilt also breaks our relationships. It's a natural tendency to avoid people we've wronged. Have you ever experienced the discomfort that comes from having someone you have gossiped about with your friends suddenly appear and attempt to join your group? Or how anxious are you to attend a family gathering that includes a relative to whom you still owe money? When is the last time you picked up the phone and called someone with whom you had a knock-down argument? Guilt produces separation.

The same phenomenon occurs in our relationship with God. As Isaiah the prophet said, "But your iniquities have made a separation between you and your God" (Isaiah 59:2). Whenever we know that we've deviated from God's standard in our lives, we instinctively run from Him. That's why it's imperative that we learn how to deal with guilt constructively.

In 1 Timothy 1:18-19, Paul includes "a good conscience" along with faith as one of two essentials for the Christian life. He tells us, "Fight the good fight, keeping faith and a good conscience, which some have rejected and suffered shipwreck in regard to their faith."

Are you suffering from a guilty conscience?

Are there scenes from your past that you wish you could erase?

Has unresolved guilt caused you to keep your distance from God?

If your answer to these questions is yes, I have good news for you. Forgiveness from the past *is* possible. If you find that difficult to believe, then consider the sordid affair of David and Bathsheba. Although David was guilty of adultery and murder, he experienced God's complete forgiveness.

AN AFFAIR TO REMEMBER

David was the most outstanding of Israel's kings. Under his military and political leadership, the nation reached heights that were previously unknown. But the king became intoxicated by his own accomplishments, causing him to think he was exempt from God's standards. We find the story of his downfall in 2 Samuel 11:1-5.

> Then it happened in the spring, at the time when kings go out to battle, that David sent Joab and his servants with him and all Israel, and they destroyed the sons of Ammon and besieged Rabbah. But David stayed at Jerusalem.
>
> Now when evening came David arose from his bed and walked around on the roof of the king's house, and from the roof he saw a woman bathing; and the woman was very beautiful in appearance. So David sent and inquired about the woman. And one said, "Is this not Bathsheba, the daughter of Eliam, the wife of Uriah the Hittite?" And David sent messengers and took her, and when she came to him, he lay with her; and when she had purified herself from her uncleanness, she returned to her house. And the woman conceived; and she sent and told David, and said, "I am pregnant."

Like any king, David should have been in battle with his men instead of at home gazing out his window. I'm sure he rationalized his absence by thinking, "I'm entitled to a little leisure considering all I've done for this country. I've spent my time lugging armor in the hot

Palestinian sun. I'll let the 'little people' do that now, while I enjoy myself."

However, that night the king of Israel became just another victim of God's universal law: "Whatever a man sows, this he will also reap" (Galatians 6:7). In this case, David's sowing resulted in Bathsheba's pregnancy.

When Bathsheba delivered to David the result of her home pregnancy test, David panicked. Petrified that someone would discover his sin, he orchestrated a master cover-up plan. He would order Bathsheba's husband home from battle, thinking that surely he would want to sleep with his wife. Then everyone would conclude that Uriah had fathered Bathsheba's child. But the best-laid plans of kings sometimes fail:

> Then David said to Uriah, "Go down to your house, and wash your feet." And Uriah went out of the king's house, and a present from the king was sent out after him. But Uriah slept at the door of the king's house with all the servants of his lord, and did not go down to his house. (2 Samuel 11:8-9)

Uriah had more integrity than his boss. He reasoned that if the men under his command were unable to enjoy sex with their wives back home, he should set a good example by restricting his own pleasure. (Don't you just hate it when people under your authority — like employees or children — show you up like that?)

David now was overcome by panic. He had to resort to Plan B. No more Mr. Nice Guy. Desperate times call for desperate measures. So David devised a scheme to have Uriah killed.

> Now it came about in the morning that David wrote a letter to Joab, and sent it by the hand of Uriah. And he had written in the letter, saying, "Place Uriah in the front line of the fiercest battle and withdraw from him, so that he may be struck down and die."...
>
> Now when the wife of Uriah heard that Uriah her husband was dead, she mourned for her husband. When the time of mourning was over, David sent and brought her to his house and she became his wife; then she bore him a son. (11:14-15, 26-27)

David thought his secret was safe. "What a clever guy I am. No wonder they made me king." But there was a problem. "The thing that David had done was evil in the sight of the LORD" (11:27).

Days, weeks, months elapsed without David experiencing any consequences for his sin. "I'm still king, and the nation is still prospering. Maybe this affair was not such a big deal after all. Maybe God doesn't care."

Unfortunately, David made the mistake that many of us make — confusing God's patience with God's tolerance. If you're living apart from God right now and haven't experienced any major calamity in your life, don't misread the situation. The only reason God has delayed His judgment is to give you an opportunity to repent.

Some years ago a Christian leader I know was engaged in a compromising relationship. He was sure that no one knew about his daily conversations and clandestine meetings with the other woman. The fact that his behavior went undetected only emboldened him to even more frequent contact with the other person. What he didn't know was that the leaders of his organization knew everything. In fact, they had set a date to confront him and dismiss him if he did not first acknowledge and repent of his misbehavior. Unfortunately this leader made the deadly mistake of confusing patience with tolerance and ended up losing his position. Solomon wisely observed,

> Because the sentence against an evil deed is not executed quickly, therefore the hearts of the sons of men among them are given fully to do evil. (Ecclesiastes 8:11)

ENTER THE PROPHET

But just as the Christian leaders' board had set a date to confront him, so God had appointed a time to expose David. After six months had elapsed, the prophet Nathan paid a visit to the king.

The old man related to David the tale of a troubling incident. A wealthy man had stolen the only possession of a poor man, a little ewe lamb, and had served it for dinner. When David heard the story of this great injustice in his own kingdom he cried out,

> As the LORD lives, surely the man who has done this deserves to die. And he must make restitution for the lamb fourfold, because he did this thing and had no compassion. (2 Samuel 12:5-6)

Mark it down: The more angry people become over the sins of others, the more guilty they usually are.

After a dramatic pause, Nathan pointed his bony finger at David and said, "You are the man." In an instant, what had been done in secret was now public knowledge.

David had a choice to make. He could continue to deny his

transgression, or he could confess it. He could either continue to cover his tracks, or he could allow God to cover his sin. Exhausted from the unrelenting guilt of the past half year, David chose the latter.

> Then David said to Nathan, "I have sinned against the LORD." And Nathan said to David, "The LORD also has taken away your sin; you shall not die." (12:13)

Psalm 51 — with a beginning inscription that reads, "A psalm of David, when Nathan the prophet came to him, after he had gone into Bathsheba" — records his fuller confession, including these words:

> Be gracious to me, O God, according to Thy loving-
> kindness;
> According to the greatness of Thy compassion blot out
> my transgressions.
> Wash me thoroughly from my iniquity
> And cleanse me from my sin.
> For I know my transgressions,
> And my sin is ever before me.
> Against Thee, Thee only, I have sinned,
> And done what is evil in Thy sight,
> So that Thou art justified when Thou dost speak,
> And blameless when Thou dost judge.
> (51:1-4)

Besides requesting to have his sin washed away and to be given "a clean heart" (51:10), David also asked God to let him experience "joy and gladness," the renewal of "a steadfast spirit within me," and the restoration of "the joy of Thy salvation" (51:8,10,12).

David's words in Psalm 32 may well reflect God's answer to this prayer, as David experienced the relief that accompanies forgiveness:

> How blessed is he whose transgression is forgiven,
> Whose sin is covered!
> How blessed is the man to whom the LORD does not
> impute iniquity,
> And in whose spirit there is no deceit!
> (32:1-2)

Are you tired of running from the past? Would you like to experience the same kind of relief that David felt when he received God's outrageous grace? Fortunately, David not only describes his own experience, but he also has outlined for us some simple, but crucial steps for receiving God's forgiveness.

1. Honestly Evaluate Your Relationship with God

Forgiveness requires a subject. Before we can be released from our guilt, we must first ask God to reveal to us where we've failed to meet His standards. David prayed,

> Search me, O God, and know my heart;
> Try me and know my anxious thoughts;
> And see if there be any hurtful way in me,
> And lead me in the everlasting way.
> (Psalm 139:23-24)

David was asking God to shine the searchlight of His spirit into every corner of his life to reveal any failure. As you pray the same kind of prayer, ask God to reveal to you where you have failed in each of these areas:

Your relationship with God — unconfessed sin, unkept promises, failure to nurture a relationship with Him.

Your relationship with your parents or siblings — ingratitude or unresolved conflicts.

Your relationship with your spouse — harsh words, selfish attitudes, or ingratitude.

Your relationship with your children — failure to spend time with them or to provide spiritual leadership for them.

Your relationship with others — immoral relationships, people whom you have offended, friendships that need to be more Christ-centered.

Your habits — immoral or slothful habits that are displeasing to God.

Your possessions — trusting in money, dishonest business dealings, failure to be a good steward.

2. Acknowledge Your Failure to God

David makes a curious comment in Psalm 51:4 — "Against Thee, Thee only, I have sinned, and done what is evil in Thy sight." Some have mistakenly assumed that such a statement reveals David's lack of repentance, since in truth he had wronged Bathsheba, Uriah, his family, and the entire nation. But I believe David's statement simply illustrates his understanding that all sin is ultimately an offense toward God. If we're going to experience forgiveness, we must first determine whom we've offended the most. And at the top of everyone's list should be God.

When you acknowledge your areas of failure to God, you're not telling Him something He doesn't already know. When you confess your sins, God doesn't slap His forehead and say, "You did *that!* I can't believe it!" God is not some ogre in heaven with a two-by-four, waiting to knock us over the head the moment we come into His presence with an admission of guilt. Instead, He's like the waiting father in the story of the prodigal son, scanning the horizon looking for any sign of our coming home.

3. Receive God's Forgiveness

God *delights* in offering forgiveness. Read again David's opening requests in Psalm 51 and notice the words used to describe God's character:

> Be gracious to me, O God, according to Thy loving-
> kindness;
> According to the greatness of Thy compassion blot out
> my transgressions.

Although God hates sin, He loves to forgive sin, a truth that flows from His abundant grace, loving-kindness, and compassion.

And His character never changes. God doesn't offer forgiveness "For a Limited Time Only, While Quantities Last." Forgiveness is always available to those who ask for it. Remember 1 John 1:9?

> If we confess our sins, He is faithful and righteous to forgive us our sins and to cleanse us from all unrighteousness.

The forgiveness described here is not the one-time act of salvation that takes place when we trust in Christ as our Savior. Instead, John is describing forgiveness for sins we commit *after* we become a Christian. Although such sins never cause us to lose our place in God's family, they do cause a rupture in our familial relationship with our Father. How? Sin always produces guilt. And guilt always breaks our relationship with another person.

Last week my daughter Dorothy presented me with her first-grade report card. The left side showed all A's. The right-hand side had a straight line of S's for her satisfactory conduct. "Dad, those are the same thing as A's," she was quick to point out.

My mind wandered back to the time I received my first report card. I'll never forget the horror I felt seeing all of those S's on the card. I knew that A was the best you could do, and the further you proceeded down the alphabet, the worse it got. If F was enough to fail you, I imagined that an S was enough to imprison you.

For the next three days I hid my report card from my parents. I remember feeling so uncomfortable with them during those days, avoiding them whenever possible. Why? Because I felt guilty. Guilt broke our relationship, even though they weren't angry with me.

If you're God's child, He may be displeased with your disobedience, but He isn't angry with you. He stands with outstretched hands ready to forgive if you will simply ask.

4. Refuse to Allow Satan to Paralyze You with Guilt

Once you have received forgiveness, you can expect Satan to continue to accuse you. You'll be trying to move past your sin, and Satan will grab you by the nape of the neck and say, "Where do you think you're going? Don't you remember what you've done? Why do you think God can use you?"

Whenever those guilt feelings come back, remember the extent of

God's forgiveness. Although God doesn't forget our sin, He covers over it completely. David expressed that truth in Psalm 51 when he prayed, "Hide Thy face from my sins, and *blot out* all my iniquities" (51:9).

The apostle Paul used another analogy to explain the completeness of God's forgiveness. In Paul's day, if you were incarcerated for a crime, a certificate was placed over your cell listing your offenses. It was called a "certificate of debt." Look what happens to our certificate of debt when we're forgiven:

> And when you were dead in your transgressions and the uncircumcision of your flesh, He made you alive together with Him, having forgiven us all our transgressions, having canceled out the certificate of debt consisting of decrees against us and which was hostile to us; and He has taken it out of the way, having nailed it to the cross. (Colossians 2:13-14)

Our debt certificate has been nailed to the cross! Our obligation has now become Christ's obligation, and He's more than willing to assume it. That's why Jesus cried out on the cross, "It is finished" (John 19:30). The word "finished" in that verse literally means "paid in full." The death of Christ accomplished what nothing else could — the complete and final payment for our sins.

RECEIVING FORGIVENESS FROM OTHERS

I have some good news and some bad news for you. Ready?

The good news is that God forgives us instantly and completely whenever we ask.

The bad news? People aren't like God.

Receiving God's forgiveness is easy; receiving other people's forgiveness can be difficult. Some would use David's statement, "Against Thee only have I sinned," as an excuse not to be overly concerned about seeking other people's forgiveness. But as we saw earlier, God desires that Christians enjoy unity with one another. Guilt severs that unity, but forgiveness can restore it.

Paul declared that his goal in life was "to maintain always a blameless conscience both before God and before men" (Acts 24:16). I like this definition for a clear conscience: "the ability to look any person in the eye and know that there is no wrong that you have not attempted to make right."[1] Whenever you wrong someone, that person holds an "account receivable" in his hands. He can choose to hold on to it, or he can release you from your obligation. It's his choice.

While we can't control what another person does, we always have a responsibility to seek reconciliation. Let's look at four practical steps for seeking forgiveness from others.

1. Determine If You Need to Ask Forgiveness

For years Trevor had been having lustful thoughts about his best friend's wife. Every time the two couples were together, Trevor would fantasize what it would be like to be married to Barbara.

One weekend Trevor and his wife, Angie, attended a spiritual life conference during which the speaker guided the participants through the steps of breaking "spiritual strongholds" in their lives. Realizing his lust had been such a stumbling block, Trevor determined to deal with it once and for all. He called his best friend, Rick, and scheduled an appointment to meet him and his wife.

That evening Trevor confessed his sin and asked for Rick and Barbara's forgiveness. He could tell by their reaction they were stunned and slightly embarrassed by his revelation. Barbara quickly excused herself to help the kids with their homework, and Trevor mumbled something about how "we all have weaknesses in our life."

After a perfunctory prayer, Trevor left feeling relieved that he had finally cleaned up this area of his life. However, he was more than a little surprised when Rick and Barbara refused his and Angie's invitation to dinner the next Friday night. In fact, they continued to refuse all invitations.

Finally, Rick told him the truth. "Trevor, we're glad you've dealt with this issue in your life. But as friends I think we can be honest. Barbara is uncomfortable around you, and we think it would be best if we didn't see each other for a while."

Trevor was both shocked and hurt. He had been sincere and transparent with them. Why couldn't they find it in their heart to forgive him?

Trevor had broken one of the cardinal rules of forgiveness: *We're to seek forgiveness only from those we have wronged.* While Trevor's lustful thoughts were certainly a sin against God that needed to be confessed to Him, they represented no real offense against Barbara — not yet, anyway.

Jesus taught that we should seek reconciliation only with those we've injured:

> If therefore you are presenting your offering at the altar, and there remember that *your brother has something against you,* leave your offering there before the altar, and go your way; first be reconciled to your brother, and then come and present your offering. (Matthew 5:23-24)

Many people misread and, therefore, misapply these verses. I've actually heard people use this verse as an excuse for skipping church. "I can't worship in the same church as my offender until he asks for my forgiveness." But Jesus is not addressing the *offended,* but the *offenders.* He pictures a worshiper deep in prayer who suddenly remembers someone he has wronged. Please note that the person from whom we seek reconciliation is someone who "has something against you" — a person who's *aware* of our offense.

I'm frequently asked this thorny question: "Should I confess an adulterous relationship to my spouse if he or she is unaware of it?" There's no easy answer here. Some would argue that since guilt breaks a relationship, confession of adultery is necessary to restore unity in a marriage. Others would argue that confessing a hidden sin may do even more damage to the relationship.

Obviously, all sin needs to be confessed to God. "He who conceals his transgressions will not prosper" (Proverbs 28:13). But what about other people we've wronged? Are there any circumstances in which we should keep our sins to ourselves?

Let me suggest a checklist for determining whether to ask forgiveness from those who are unaware of your actions:

Is restitution necessary? If your employer is aware of money you've stolen, you have an obligation to confess your offense in order to return the money.

What are the chances your offense will be discovered? An affair that took place thirty years ago may never come to light in your marriage now. However, a relationship that occurred six months ago may very likely come to your mate's attention. Hearing the news from someone else would be more hurtful than hearing it from you.

Will your confession help or hurt the other party? This is the bottom-line issue. Sometimes our desire to "confess" can be very self-centered. While we may feel relieved after unloading our garbage on our spouse, he or she may be devastated. Sometimes sacrificial love entails our willingness to bear our own burdens instead of asking someone else to share the load.

Scripture gives us a great filter to use for *all* our words to another person, including confessions:

> Let no unwholesome word proceed from your mouth,
> but only such a word as is good for edification according
> to the need of the moment, that it may give grace to
> those who hear. (Ephesians 4:29)

Before you confess a hidden offense such as adultery, ask yourself if your admission will edify — build up — or tear down the other party.

2. Schedule an Appointment to Meet the Offended Party

Once you've determined that there's someone or a group of people whose forgiveness you need, you should arrange a face-to-face meeting.

Remember, your circle of confession should be no larger than your circle of offense. A member of a church I served was involved in an activity that injured the witness of our fellowship, and he correctly sought forgiveness from the entire congregation. But if you've offended one individual, then you need to confess your fault only to God and that person. While group confessionals are popular in some circles, restricting your confession to those you've offended is a biblical principle. James wrote:

> Therefore, confess your sins to *one another,* and pray *for*
> *one another,* so that you may be healed. (James 5:16)

A personal meeting is certainly the preferred method of communication. When you try to arrange such a meeting, I would suggest you say to the person, "There's something important I need to discuss with you. Could I meet you at [time] at [location]?" My experience has been that often the other party will try to pry out of you the reason for the meeting. Instead of revealing that reason, simply say, "This is something so important that I'd rather talk with you in person when we have enough time."

If it's impossible to meet with the offended party in person, the telephone is the next best method. The major drawback of the telephone is its inability to communicate facial expressions and body language. The other party needs to be able to sense your sincerity and remorse. Likewise, you need to be able to gauge his or her response to your request for forgiveness.

The least preferred method of communication is a letter. As someone once said, the reason for asking forgiveness is to *erase* the past, not *document* it! Obviously, without the ability to hear the tone of our voice, see our facial responses, or ask follow-up questions, another person could easily misinterpret our written words on a page.[2]

I encourage you to make whatever sacrifice necessary to a personal meeting as quickly as possible. This business of a clear conscience is so important that, as you'll recall, Jesus commands us to drop whatever we're doing, including worshiping God, in order to be reunited with an offended party: "Leave your offering there before the altar, and go your way; first be reconciled to your brother, and then come and present your offering" (Matthew 5:24).

I remember hearing Chuck Swindoll relate how he had heard that another person was accusing him of some personal offenses. Chuck was so disturbed about the matter that he got on an airplane and traveled to another city to seek that person's forgiveness. The time and sacrifice required for such an effort may seem high, but it is negligible compared to the joy of a clear conscience.

3. Ask for the Other Person's Forgiveness

Recently we've been trying to teach our two daughters how to effectively ask for forgiveness after one of them has lashed out at the other. Once Mom or Dad has apprehended the guilty party, we say, "Now you need to ask your sister for forgiveness." Reluctantly (and unconvincingly), the errant sister mutters "Sorry" and runs from the room. The offended party is understandably unmoved by her sister's contrition.

Children aren't the only ones who need to learn how to ask for forgiveness. Seeking forgiveness should never be confused with making an apology. An apology is a unilateral (one-sided) response to an offense. Apologies can be filled with genuine remorse ("Words could never express how terrible I feel for running over your cat"), or they can simply be a bare acknowledgment of the possibility of wrongdoing ("I admit I may have made mistakes in our marriage.")

While seeking forgiveness certainly includes an admission of guilt, it involves much more than that. Requesting forgiveness is asking the person you've wronged *to do something:* to release you from your obligation.

Remember the slave in Jesus' story who owed his master five billion dollars? When he was brought before the king, did he nonchalantly say, "I owe you some money — sorry," then stroll out of the palace? No, he desperately wanted release from his debt:

> The slave therefore falling down, prostrated himself before him, saying, "Have patience with me, and I will repay you everything." (Matthew 18:26)

The slave understood that he owed the king a tremendous debt, and he begged for mercy. While prostrating yourself before another person may be a little extreme, there are essential guidelines for effectively asking for forgiveness:

Refuse to blame others. The confession that begins, "You know, both of us share some blame for this problem, and I'm willing to accept my share if you will," is doomed from the beginning. Even if the other person is largely responsible for the conflict, you need to concentrate on *your* offense.

Identify the wrong you've committed. Don't try to minimize your offense by confessing only minor transgressions. A person guilty of incest who says to the innocent party, "I'm sorry I haven't been the kind of [father, uncle, etc.] I should have been," is not dealing with the real issue and will only compound the resentment. Remember, the other person is already aware of what *you've* done; now he or she wants to know that *you* are fully aware of it.

Acknowledge the hurt you've caused. The other party wants to know that you understand the pain that he or she has suffered because of your actions. Try and relive your offense through that person's eyes. Recently a staff member who had disappointed me said, "I can't imagine the grief and embarrassment this must have caused you. I'm sure my mistake has kept you awake at nights and distracted you from doing your job. Will you please forgive me?" Such an understanding will make the other party much more likely to forgive.

Ask the other person to forgive you. Remember again that forgiveness is a transaction in which the other party voluntarily releases you from your offense. To end your discussion without asking for such a release is harmful both of you. He needs to forgive as much as you need to be forgiven. However, it's imperative that you not demand forgiveness or even imply he should forgive for his own benefit. Instead, you might use wording such as this: "I realize that I've wronged you by ___________. I'll do my best to see that I never do this again, though I realize there's nothing I can do to erase the deep pain I've caused you. What I did was wrong, and I can blame no one but myself. I'm coming to you today asking if you could find it in your heart to forgive me for what I've done."

4. Be Prepared for a Negative Response

Not every attempt at reconciliation results in a warm embrace and a happy ending. The other party may respond ambivalently ("I don't know. I'll have to think about it.") or even negatively ("You think a simple apology can erase all the pain *you've* cause me? Forget it.") Such a response can be especially hurtful after *you've* poured out your heart to the other person.

Why do people refuse to forgive? The other party may be reluctant to forgive because:

He doesn't sense that you're remorseful. Attaching blame to others, lack of identifying the real offense, improper voice inflections, or failing to understand the hurt inflicted are just some of the ways we demonstrate insincerity in our request for forgiveness.

He feels guilty himself. Remember the guilt-blame seesaw? If the other person is partly to blame for the offense or feels guilt about some other area in his life, he may find it difficult to release you from your obligation. Why? It's much easier to handle our own guilt if we can balance it with blame toward another.

He wants restitution. Someone may be willing to forgive us for stealing a hundred dollars from him, but before forgiving us, he'll want to make sure we intend to return the money.

He fears a repetition of the offense. Remember that genuine repentance involves a willingness to turn away from unacceptable behavior. Before the other party releases us from our guilt, he'll want evidence that we have indeed made such a change.

He confuses forgiveness with reconciliation. The abused wife may be reluctant to forgive her husband if she assumes that granting forgiveness means automatically giving him a key to the front door. The wronged church may find it difficult to forgive the fallen minister if members confuse granting forgiveness with rehiring the leader. Remember, forgiveness is *granted,* but reconciliation is *earned.*

Even if the other party refuses to forgive you immediately, don't be discouraged. Sometimes the wounds we inflict on others are quite deep. The other person may need time before he can grant forgiveness. Occasionally, the other party will never be willing to forgive — which is tragic, since forgiveness is the only way to heal those deep wounds.

But whether or not the other party forgives, there is freedom in having a clear conscience — knowing that neither God nor any other person can accuse you of a wrong you have never attempted to make right.

CHAPTER 9

GRANTING THE GIFT

The three-step process for letting go of poisonous people in your life

There's a story about the man bitten by a dog that was later discovered to have rabies. The man was rushed to the hospital where tests revealed that he, too, had contracted the dreaded disease. At the time, medical science had not discovered a cure for rabies, so the doctor had the difficult task of informing his patient that his condition was both incurable and terminal.

"Sir, we'll do all we can to make you comfortable, but I suggest that you quickly get your affairs in order," the doctor advised.

The dying man sank back on his bed in shock. After a few minutes he summoned the strength to ask for a pen and paper. He then began to write with great energy.

An hour later the doctor stopped by to check up on his patient, who was continuing to write vigorously.

"I'm glad to see you're working on your will," the doctor said.

"This ain't no will," the man answered. "This is a list of all the people I'm going to bite before I die!"[1]

My years as a pastor have led me to believe that most of us carry such a list around — if not in our pockets, certainly in our hearts. Your list might include a family member who has wronged you, a business associate who has cheated you, a child who has disappointed you, a friend who has betrayed you, or a mate who has deserted you.

Deep down you want to see these people suffer for the pain they've caused you. The Bible labels that desire vengeance, and vengeance that is harbored long enough eventually becomes bitterness. Sometimes bitterness erupts into the violent actions we read about in the newspaper — an angry husband murders his entire family, a student jilted by his girlfriend climbs a tower and randomly shoots at passing students, a terminated employee returns to the office to gun down his former coworkers.

But more often bitterness works like a cancer, slowly destroying everything it touches. That's why the writer of Hebrews warns us:

> See to it that no one comes short of the grace of God;
> that no root of bitterness springing up causes trouble, and
> by it many be defiled. (Hebrews 12:15)

If holding on to vengeance — our desire to see our offender suffer — is the root cause of bitterness, then doesn't it make sense that the antidote to bitterness is releasing that desire? That's the essence of forgiveness. The word "forgive" means to release our desire (and right) for vengeance.

As we saw earlier, there are many reasons to chose forgiveness over vengeance:

1. Forgiveness is the only way to settle a debt.
2. Forgiveness frees us to get on with our lives.

3. Forgiveness is an antidote to needless suffering.
4. Forgiveness is the obligation of the forgiven.

While all four reasons are strong arguments for unconditionally forgiving another person, let's concentrate for a moment on the third truth: Forgiveness is an antidote to needless suffering.

I've recently been counseling with a wife who discovered her husband had been involved in an affair. She and her husband had what many would consider an ideal marriage: They were always holding hands in public, they ate lunch together twice a week, and they enjoyed frequent romantic weekend getaways.

But one Friday afternoon her tranquil life turned into a living nightmare. Her best friend reluctantly informed her that her husband had been involved in a yearlong romance with a mutual friend. When she confronted her husband, he first denied the relationship, but later confessed.

He genuinely wants their marriage to continue, but his wife is understandably devastated. "I don't know if I can ever forgive him," she told me. "I just keep picturing him and this woman in bed together. I would give anything if we could erase this past year and start over."

But of course she can't. The wounds of the past can never be changed. But they can be healed, and forgiveness is a procedure God has given us to accomplish that physical, emotional, and spiritual renewal in our lives.

Perhaps you remember the events of a March day in 1981 when President Ronald Reagan was shot by would-be assassin John Hinckley. His daughter, Patti Davis, relates the story of her father's remarkable recovery after sustaining this life-threatening injury:

> [My father] said he knew that his physical healing was directly dependent on his ability to forgive John

> Hinckley. Forgiveness is hard work, but my father made it sound effortless.
>
> Many times I'd listened to my father tell me that we are all God's children. Maybe at one time I chalked it up to the language of a churchgoing man. But when he referred to John Hinckley as "misguided," I felt the weight of that word — the weight of what it said about my father. He never expressed hatred for the man who had shot him. He expressed pity. He knew in his world that even Hinckley belonged to God. That knowledge leads to forgiveness; it transforms and heals.[2]

In this chapter we're going to learn how to forgive others for the deep wounds of past offenses and — in the process — how to experience transforming healing for ourselves.

A FORGIVENESS CHAMPION

No story in human history better illustrates the process of granting forgiveness than the story of Joseph and his brothers. Let's briefly review his remarkable life.

The Offense

Joseph was one of Jacob's twelve sons. In fact, he was Jacob's favorite son, as evidenced by that famous multicolored coat his dad bestowed upon him. You can probably understand why Joseph did not enjoy "most-favored brother status" among his siblings, especially when he unwisely told them about his dream that he would one day rule over them.

One day Jacob dispatched Joseph to check on his brothers, who were far away tending the sheep. When Joseph finally found them, he did not receive a cordial welcome. Instead, his brothers insisted on killing him, but ultimately compromised on selling him into slavery. After dipping Joseph's coat in animal blood, the brothers returned it to their father with the story that a wild animal had killed his favorite son. Upon hearing the news, "Jacob tore his clothes…and mourned for his son many days" (Genesis 37:34).

Forsaken but Not Forgotten

Through a long series of miraculous circumstances in Egypt, God elevated Joseph from slavery to becoming Pharaoh's right-hand man.

Once Joseph had risen to this position, God revealed to Pharaoh (through a dream only Joseph could interpret) that there would be seven years of plentiful harvest in Egypt, followed by seven years of famine. Joseph wisely advised Pharaoh to stockpile excess grain during the first seven years to prepare for the coming shortage.

Just as God predicted, the seven years of famine engulfed not only Egypt, but also Canaan, where Joseph's family resided. When Jacob heard that there was food in Egypt, he sent his sons to purchase grain in Egypt. Little did they know that the person to whom they would make their appeal would be their own brother.

The Confrontation

Genesis 45 records the climactic confrontation between Joseph and his brothers:

> Then Joseph could not control himself before all those who stood by him, and he cried, "Have everyone go out

> from me." So there was no man with him when Joseph made himself known to his brothers. And he wept so loudly that the Egyptians heard it, and the household of Pharaoh heard of it. Then Joseph said to his brothers, "I am Joseph! Is my father still alive?" But his brothers could not answer him, for they were dismayed at his presence. Then Joseph said to his brothers, "Please come closer to me." And they came closer. (45:1-4)

As the shock wore off, can you imagine what the brothers must have been thinking? "This is it! Surely Joseph will get even with us now!" With sweat pouring down the faces, they slowly approached their brother, certain that this was the end. Never in their wildest dreams could they have anticipated Joseph's remarkable response:

> I am your brother Joseph, whom you sold into Egypt. And now do not be grieved or angry with yourselves, because you sold me here; for God sent me before you to preserve life.... And God sent me before you to preserve for you a remnant in the earth, and to keep you alive by a great deliverance. Now, therefore, it was not you who sent me here, but God.... Hurry and go up to my father, and say to him, "Thus says your son Joseph, 'God has made me lord of all Egypt; come down to me, do not delay.'" (Genesis 45:4-5,7-9)

Jacob and his sons accepted Joseph's invitation and settled in the fertile region of Goshen in the land of Egypt, where they enjoyed once more the benefits of a reunited family.

Any student of the Bible might wonder why the book of Genesis devotes more space to Joseph's life than to Adam and Eve, the first couple, or to Noah, the hero of the ark and the flood, or to Abraham, father of the Jewish nation. I believe the answer is that Joseph illustrates one of life's most important choices: the choice to forgive.

Think for a moment what would have happened if Joseph had *not* forgiven his brothers. Imagine that when his brothers came requesting grain, Joseph had answered, "You want food? Funny you should mention that. Just today I was thinking about how much *I* wanted food when you left me for dead in that stinking pit."

Had Joseph held on to his desire for vengeance and allowed his brothers to starve to death, the lasting consequences would have reverberated throughout eternity. Instead, Joseph's remarkable story not only ensured the development of the nation of Israel, from whom Jesus Christ would come to save the world, but also serves as an inspiration and illustration for how we're to bestow true forgiveness upon others.

True Forgiveness Admits That Someone Has Wronged You

How often have you heard the following advice: "Stop playing the blame game. Instead of concentrating on what other people have done to you, focus on the wrongs *you* have committed"? Such counsel, while sounding pious, is actually lethal to the process of true forgiveness. You cannot forgive another person without first acknowledging that they've wronged you. Lewis Smedes writes: "We do not excuse the person we forgive; we blame the person we forgive."[3]

Joseph understood the importance of assigning blame to his brothers. In his confrontation with them he did not act like a Pollyanna by saying, "Now guys, I know you didn't mean to sell me into slavery. You were probably just having a bad day. Let's forget this ever happened."

Nor does he acknowledge his own partial responsibility for his childhood conflict with them by saying, "Brothers, there's enough blame to share among all of us. Let's allow bygones to be bygones and try and start over." Instead, Joseph is painfully direct: "You meant evil against me." Joseph was saying in effect, "What you did to me was inexcusable. You and you alone are to blame for the years of unjust suffering I endured."

Nor did such a statement reveal unresolved bitterness in his life. With his next words — "but God meant it for good" — Joseph showed that he was focused not on his brothers' offenses, but on God's sovereignty over the situation. Nevertheless, Joseph understood that we cannot forgive people we aren't willing to blame.

In the same way, before you can forgive someone, you must first identify *who* and *what* you're forgiving. You must admit (at least to yourself) that an injustice has occurred.

True Forgiveness Acknowledges That a Debt Exists

Wrongs create obligations. A traffic violation results in a fine. A guilty verdict results in a sentence. A broken curfew results in grounding. Sin results in eternal death — "For the wages of sin is death" (Romans 6:23). Usually we think of wages positively, but Paul uses the term negatively: Because of our sin we have "earned" eternal separation from God. Wrongs result in an indebtedness.

Joseph not only admitted that his brothers wronged him, but that they *owed* him for what they had done. When Joseph said, "Do not be afraid" (Genesis 50:19), he was implying that they had every reason to be afraid! They deserved the death sentence for what they had done, and with a simple nod Joseph could have had them executed. Before either we or our offender can appreciate the freedom that comes from forgiveness, we must first understand the obligation that accrues from our offense.

Yesterday morning I was in a hurry to get to work and was doing about seventy miles per hour when I sailed past a patrolman. I'm not sure he noticed me. Or perhaps he did notice me and even recognized me and decided that this was "Be Nice to a Speeding Pastor Day" and let me off the hook.

But suppose the patrolman had turned on his lights and siren and stopped me. He would have reminded me of the speed limit for that stretch of road, then informed me to what degree I had violated that, as well as the penalty for such a violation. He might then have continued, "Although I should throw the book at you, I'm going to let you go this time. However, if I ever catch you speeding again —" But before "forgiving" me of my violation and deserved penalty, he would still have made it clear what that violation and penalty were.

Before we can properly forgive another person, we must accurately assess what he or she owes us.

When you think of the word *forgive,* does someone's name immediately come to your mind? In addition to identifying exactly what that person has done to you, I encourage you to calculate the debt he or she owes you for that wrong. Be as severe as you think you need to be.

"Because of your affair, I should divorce you."

"Because of your negligence, I should sue you."

"Because of your actions, I should prosecute you."

Remember, offenses always create obligations.

True Forgiveness Releases Our Offender of His or Her Obligation

Only after we've identified the offense committed and calculated the debt owed can we truly forgive the other person. Remember that the word "forgive" means to release another person of his obligation toward us, as Joseph did. Instead of giving his brothers the death sentence they most certainly deserved, he formally released them from their debt by giving them a new land that they did not deserve:

> And you shall live in the land of Goshen, and you shall be near me, you and your children and your children's children and your flocks and your herds and all that you have. (Genesis 45:10)

In the same way, there needs to be a specific time when you formally release your offender of his obligation toward you. Whether or not you chose to voice your forgiveness to your offender, you can express it to God. Visualize in your mind the person who has wronged you. Admit to God that you've been hurt — deeply hurt — by what he or she has done to you. Calculate what that person owes you for the offense: money, separation, divorce, jail, or maybe death. Finally, let me encourage you to pray something like this: "What ______ did to me was wrong, and he should pay for what he did. But today I'm releasing him of his obligation to me. Not because he deserves it, or has even asked for my forgiveness, but because You, God, have released me from the debt I owe You."

True Forgiveness Waits for the Right Time to Confront Our Offender

Throughout this book we've seen that forgiveness is a unilateral action that I can take. However, before I can ever be reunited with my offender, he must desire my forgiveness. While forgiveness depends upon me, reconciliation depends upon *us.*

In Joseph's example, we see an extended period of time — represented in an intricate series of events portrayed in Genesis 42–44 — between the day Joseph first encountered his brothers in Egypt and the day he finally revealed himself to them.

I'm convinced that from the first moment he saw them, Joseph began planning for their ultimate reunion. Such a desire for reconciliation comes only from those who have truly chosen forgiveness. But Joseph was full of wisdom as well as grace. He understood that only those who are truly repentant can receive forgiveness, so he waited for the right time to confront his offenders. Joseph longed for more than just the personal freedom that comes from forgiveness. He wanted to be reconciled with his family. And before they could achieve that reunion, he had to determine whether his brothers were truly repentant.

Before you verbally offer forgiveness to your offender, make sure he's ready to receive it. Look for the following clues:

Does he demonstrate any remorse for what he has done?

Is he willing to speak to you, or does he avoid you?

Has he given any hints that he's interested in reconciling with you?

Does he demonstrate any evidence of change in his life?

While repentance isn't necessary for granting forgiveness, it is vital for receiving forgiveness. Augustine once said, "God gives where He finds empty hands. A man whose hands are full of parcels can't receive a gift."

HAVE YOU REALLY FORGIVEN YOUR OFFENDER?

If you sense that your offender is open to reconciliation and you chose to verbalize your forgiveness, you may want to follow Joseph's example. In fact, consider the following additional suggestions not only as guidelines but as a three-point checklist to determine whether you've really forgiven you offender.

True Forgiveness Resists Unnecessary Embarrassment

Before Joseph revealed himself to his brothers, he had all of his Egyptian servants leave the room (Genesis 45:1). Why the secrecy? Joseph was trying to protect his brothers from unnecessary embarrassment. Knowing that his brothers would be living in Egypt a long time, Joseph sought to keep their offenses as private as possible instead of allowing the news to spread through the Egyptian grapevine.

Obviously there are times when offenses have to be reported to others. However, if we've truly forgiven another person, we'll try and keep their sin as confidential as possible.

True Forgiveness Relieves People of Unhealthy Sorrow

We've seen that there are two types of sorrow that accompany sin: a godly kind of sorrow that leads to change and an unhealthy sorrow that leads to paralyzing self-pity. If we've sincerely forgiven someone, we'll attempt to relieve him of unhealthy remorse.

However, that isn't nearly as much fun as watching our offender buckle under a weight of guilt. As Chuck Swindoll says, "We would much rather sit on a judgment seat than on a mercy seat. If somebody hurts us we would much rather see him squirm in misery than smile in relief."

Such a desire to see our offender squirm is not forgiveness but vengeance. By contrast, Joseph chose to sit on the mercy seat and relieve his brothers of their unhealthy grief. He told them, "And now do not be grieved or angry with yourselves, because you sold me here; for God sent me before you to preserve life" (Genesis 45:5).

True Forgiveness Continually Releases Our Offender of His or Her Obligation

Years after Joseph's initial confrontation with his brothers in Egypt, he had to face the forgiveness issue again.

When their father Jacob finally died at the age of 147, Joseph's brothers again began to worry. Could Joseph's forgiving spirit simply have been a charade to appease their aged father? Now that dear old dad was gone, might Joseph unleash his vengeance against his siblings?

In a preemptive strike, the brothers decided to butter up their brother. They "came and fell down before him and said, 'Behold, we are your servants'" (Genesis 50:18).

But Joseph saw right through them. Sensing their overwhelming fear, he comforted them with these reassuring words:

> "Do not be afraid, for am I in God's place? And as for you, you meant evil against me, but God meant it for good in order to bring about this present result, to preserve many people alive. So therefore, do not be afraid; I will provide for you and your little ones." So he comforted them and spoke kindly to them. (Genesis 50:19-21)

Forgiveness isn't a one-time action of the heart, but a continual choice of the will. As someone said, "Forgiveness is surrendering the right to hurt you for hurting me."

What was Joseph's motivation in forgiving his brothers? Why was he willing to let go of such a deep and inexcusable wrong?

Joseph was a man of faith who was able to trace the hand of God in every hurt he had experienced. He could see how God had caused all things "to work together for good." While understanding God's sovereignty facilitated Joseph's forgiveness, it doesn't explain it completely.

I think Joseph had a much more "selfish" reason for releasing his desire for vengeance. He was tired of the solitary confinement that comes from bitterness. Years of estrangement had taken their toll. Joseph desperately yearned for reconciliation with his family. Notice how his pent-up emotions erupted when he finally revealed himself to his brothers:

> And he wept so loudly that the Egyptians heard it, and the household of Pharaoh heard of it. (Genesis 45:2)

Such tears come only from those who are tired of rehearsing wrongs from the past and are ready to repair broken relationships.

Are you tired of being emotionally bound to someone who hurt you so long ago? Do you long to be free from that bitterness that has been slowly destroying your life?

Admit that you've been hurt.

Acknowledge the debt you are owed.

And release your offender of his obligation, knowing that in the process you're also releasing yourself.

CHAPTER 10

FORGIVING GOD?

Why blaming God for your problems makes more sense than you think

I've just hung up the phone after talking with a woman who desperately needs to forgive someone. The only problem is that she's not sure *whom* to forgive.

Six months ago she went to her doctor complaining of digestive disorders and sharp pains in her stomach. The doctor at that time had suggested simply that she cut back on her daily medication, which she was taking because of an earlier heart problem.

But now, after further examination, the doctor informed her that she had stomach cancer that had spread to other organs in her body. "Under the most optimistic scenario, you probably have a year to live," he told her.

The woman and her husband were understandably distraught when they talked with me. The misdiagnosis six months ago was about to rob a man of his life partner, four children of their mother, and a woman of her life.

I knew that this couple, being committed Christians, wanted to avoid the trap of resentment at any cost. They were willing to forgive — if they could only determine who was to blame for this tragedy.

Was it the doctor who failed to perform the appropriate tests six months earlier?

Themselves for not seeking a second opinion at that time?

The insurance company that recommended the doctor through their HMO?

The owners of the manufacturing company near her home that continually release pollutants in the air?

THE USUAL SUSPECTS

As we saw in the last chapter, blame is a prerequisite for forgiveness. Before we can release someone of an obligation they have to us, we must first determine who is responsible for the offense. But playing the blame game isn't always simple.

For the last several months my wife has been battling with a department store over a defective washing machine. The first machine delivered to our home had a faulty transmission and spewed oil all over our clean garments. The second one had a large dent in the front. The third machine was the wrong color. Finally, I called the store and, in my most compassionate ministerial tone, explained that we were returning the washing machine and would take our business elsewhere. The clerk assured me that my bill would be credited.

However, after several weeks no credit appeared on my statement. When I called the appliance department, the clerk swore that he had turned in the proper paperwork and that the problem was with the accounting department. A phone call to the accounting department resulted in a suggestion to check with the general manager. The general manager "couldn't imagine what the problem was" and gave me the 800-number for the national office. I had a legitimate complaint, but no one was willing to assume responsibility for it.

For a moment I want you to visualize some injustice you've suffered in life — not just a slight offense from which you recovered long ago, but some deep hurt from which you're still attempting to recover. That hurt might be

an unwanted divorce
a crippling illness
an undeserved loss of your job
a tragic accident that claimed the life of a child
a betrayal by a close friend

With that offense clearly in mind, imagine that you walk into the complaint department of your local department store. Like me, you've suffered an injustice that you want settled. But unlike me, you're willing to let go of the debt owed to you, if only you can figure out whom to forgive. In the complaint department of our imaginary store there are a number of windows you can choose.

Window Number 1: Other People

Certainly the easiest target for our blame is other people. The irresponsible doctor, the unfaithful mate, the insensitive pastor, or the disloyal friend can be held directly responsible for our suffering. The ability to link our pain to a specific face may not make forgiveness easy, but at least it makes it possible.

Throughout this book we've seen that the basis for forgiving other people is the realization of the tremendous obligation from which we've been forgiven.

> And be kind to one another, tender-hearted, forgiving each other, just as God in Christ also has forgiven you. (Ephesians 4:32)

Ron Mehl tells a great story about an eight-year-old boy who sat in class taking a test. Nervous over the exam and concerned about completing it on time, the boy wet his pants. As he looked down and saw the little puddle beneath him, he was sick with worry and embarrassment.

At that moment he looked up and saw his teacher motioning for him to come to her desk. *What am I going to do now?* he wondered.

Seeing that the boy seemed frozen in his chair, the teacher got up from her desk and started walking toward the boy. *Oh, no! She's going to discover my accident and everyone will laugh at me. This is going to be terrible!*

What the little boy couldn't see was that one of his classmates, a little girl, was coming down the aisle from behind him carrying a large fishbowl. When she got alongside him, she suddenly lurched forward, dropping the fishbowl and sending water and flying fish everywhere. The boy was suddenly covered in fish-tank water. *There really is a God in heaven! What a wonderful gift! What a wonderful girl!*

But then it dawned on him that little boys are not supposed to show any compassion for little girls. So he looked at her and said, "What's wrong with you, you clumsy clod? Why don't you watch where you're going?" The class laughed at the girl while the teacher took the little boy to the gym so that he might change into some dry clothes. At lunchtime, everyone shunned the girl. Her friends refused to play with her at recess. She was an outcast.

When the day was over, the little boy darted out of the schoolhouse on the way home. He noticed the girl walking by herself along the fence. Reflecting on what had happened to him earlier, he walked over to her.

"You know," he said, "I've been thinking about what happened today. That wasn't an accident, was it? You did that on purpose didn't you?"

"Yes," she said. "I did do it on purpose. I knew what had happened to you. You see, I wet my pants once, too."[1]

The Bible says that we've all wet our pants, so to speak. We all stand guilty and humiliated before God. But out of a deep desire to spare us from the consequences of our sin, God spilled out His blood for us so that our sins might be covered. And it's because of His willingness to suffer shame for us that we should be willing to cover over the mistakes of others.

Window Number 2: Ourselves

Sometimes we need look no farther than the mirror to find the appropriate person to blame for our suffering. Many times the injuries we sustain are self-inflicted. We may be the primary cause of a failed career, a devastating divorce, or a life-threatening illness. But even in those cases we need to learn how to forgive ourselves.

The subject of forgiving ourselves is hotly debated among the forgiveness experts. Some argue that forgiving yourself is as impossible as solitaire Ping-Pong. Just as it's impossible to be on both sides of the net at the same time, it's impossible to be on the giving and receiving end of forgiveness simultaneously. You can forgive others, but not yourself, they claim.

Perhaps that's technically true. As the scribes asked, "Who can forgive sins but God alone?" (Mark 2:7). Only those we injure can offer us absolution from our guilt. But consider a truck driver who falls asleep at the wheel and collides with an oncoming car, killing an entire family. He has certainly injured others, but hasn't he also done irreparable harm to himself? Although he may receive the forgiveness of the family's relatives and will certainly receive God's forgiveness if he asks, isn't it possible that he might still feel guilty? A thousand "if only's" might flood his mind:

If only I'd refused to work overtime.
If only I'd stopped for a cup of coffee earlier.
If only I'd pulled over for a nap instead trying to meet my schedule.

Sometimes the only way to forgive ourselves is by remembering our humanity. After we've sought forgiveness from God and those we've injured, we may still need to release ourselves from guilt by recognizing our limitations, just as God recognizes them: "For He Himself knows our frame; He is mindful that we are but dust" (Psalm 103:14).

If God is willing to accept our frailties, why can't we?

Window Number 3: Circumstances

At other times, circumstances are the source of our injuries. Our newspaper recently carried a story about a tragedy at a local amusement park that claimed the life of a young mother. A large floating inner tube carrying eight passengers capsized, trapping the passengers underneath the water. One passenger was killed and others were injured. After several months of investigation, an engineering team concluded that there was no human error involved in the accident. Instead, a list of isolated factors converged to cause the freakish mishap.

Jesus spoke of a similar incident in Luke 13:4, in which eighteen people were killed when a tower fell on them. He then asked rhetorically if these eighteen victims "were worse culprits than all the men who live in Jerusalem?" Jesus was saying that bad things happen to bad people...and to good people. Towers fall on the just and the unjust.

So whom do we blame and then forgive in these kinds of accidents? Who is responsible for —

the unexplained downturn in the economy that costs us our job
the electrical spark near the fuel tank that downs a jetliner
the maverick cell that grows into a life-threatening disease

Such questions lead some people, especially Christians, to a favorite blame target.

Window Number 4: Satan

Last night I was watching an interview on CNN with a world-famous clergyman. The interviewer asked why God would allow such things as the tragic school shootings in this country to happen. The minister replied that God was not responsible — Satan was.

I could see by the interviewer's face that he was champing at the bit to ask the natural follow-up question but decided not to press the issue. But it's a question that still needs to be asked: Couldn't God have stopped Satan if He wanted to?

The Bible teaches that Satan is the "ruler of this world" (John 12:31), the "god of this world" (2 Corinthians 4:4), and the "prince of the power of the air" (Ephesians 2:2). Nevertheless, he's not all-powerful. Satan is a created being with definite limitations. He's not the opposite of God, but the counterpart of Michael the archangel. Satan is like a junkyard dog on a very long chain. His freedom to destroy is considerable, but not unlimited. That's why he cannot be held ultimately responsible for the pain in our life.

So who *is* to blame?

LET ME SPEAK TO THE MANAGER

Last night I finally had enough of our washing machine ordeal. Tired of the runaround I was getting from my local merchant, I hopped in my car and sped to the store, bounding through the doors looking for someone to talk with.

A salesperson recognized me immediately and tried to head me off at the pass. "Dr. Jeffress, I'm doing everything I can do to clear this up." I assured her that while I appreciated her efforts, I wanted to talk to the person in charge. She suggested I might speak with the head of the appliance department, but I had no interest in that either. The only person I wanted to see was the manager of the store. He was ultimately responsible for correcting the injustice I had suffered.

Reluctantly, the salesperson escorted me to the office area. While I waited in the foyer, she buzzed him on the phone. I heard her whisper into the receiver, "No, he's *here* in person and wants to talk to you.... No, he said he will only talk with you."

After the obligatory wait to remind me who was in charge, the manager finally appeared from his office and, after endlessly tapping on the computer, finally admitted the store's error and credited my account.

The lesson I learned? When you want something settled, you need to go to the top!

The same principle applies to forgiveness. Assigning blame only to other people, yourself, circumstances, or Satan can prevent you from completing the forgiveness transaction.

After years of bitterness toward an adulterous ex-husband, Janet may finally decide to grant him forgiveness. But is he really the only culprit needing to be forgiven? Why was Janet so naive not to recognize his wandering eye during the engagement period? And what about the unfortunate external circumstances that put undue pressure on their marriage, like her back surgery last year? And didn't Satan bear some responsibility for placing that attractive coworker in her husband's office and leading him into temptation?

All of these questions are legitimate, but they mask the bottom-line question: Isn't God ultimately to blame for this? Could not God have —

harnessed her husband's sexual appetite
enlightened her earlier concerning his bent toward immorality
prevented her back injury
overridden Satan's power in her husband's life
answered her prayer for reconciliation

After all, wasn't Job right when he told God, "I know that you can do anything and that no one can stop you"? (Job 42:2, TLB).

God must be held accountable for everything that happens in His creation. After all, if His claim is true that "I am the LORD, and there is no other" (Isaiah 45:6), then He must bear the responsibility for every injustice in the universe, including the hurts we experience. That's the downside of being an all-powerful monarch. As the old saying goes, "He who calls the shots must take the shots."

Sometimes the attacks against God can be intense. Lewis Smedes retells an old story about a tailor leaving the synagogue after his daily prayers and encountering a rabbi.

"Well, what have you been doing in the synagogue, Lev Shram?" the rabbi inquires.

"I was saying prayers, Rabbi."

"That's good. And did you confess your sins?"

"Yes, Rabbi, I confessed my little sins."

"Your little sins?"

"Yes, I confessed that sometimes I cut my cloth on the short side and that I cheat on a yard of wool by a couple of inches."

"You actually said that to God?"

"Yes, Rabbi, and I said something else. 'Lord, I cheat on pieces of cloth; You let little babies die. But I'm going to make you a deal. You forgive me my little sins, and I'll forgive you Your big ones.'"[2]

I realize that the concept of "forgiving God" is offensive to some and borders on the blasphemous to others. To claim that God needs to be forgiven implies that

(a) God has sinned against us.

(b) God owes us for what He has done to us.

(c) We have the power to release God of His obligation to us.

But the Bible teaches that none of the above is possible. Consider the following verses:

> Thou art *good* and *doest good.* (Psalm 119:68)

> For we do not have a high priest who cannot sympathize with our weaknesses, but one who has been tempted in all things as we are, yet *without sin.* (Hebrews 4:15)

> Who are you, O man, who answers back to God? The thing molded will not say to the molder, "Why did you make me like this," will it? Or does not the potter have a right over the clay, to make from the same lump one vessel for honorable use, and another for common use? (Romans 9:20-21)

As I read these verses, I can understand why my editor got a little antsy over the chapter title "Forgiving God." God is incapable of sinning against His creatures and, therefore, owes us nothing. But even if He did, we're in no position to "forgive" our Creator of anything.

So instead of "Forgiving God," let's change the chapter title to "Blaming God." No, that doesn't work either, because blame implies guilt, and we've seen God is guilty of nothing. Perhaps the best title then is "Holding God Accountable." Until you're willing to allow God to assume responsibility for a failed marriage, a handicapped child, an economic hardship, or an untimely death, you will never be able to truly forgive others.

If the concept of holding God accountable for your hurts seems heretical, consider the following truths.

God's Plan for Your Life Includes Suffering

To forgive, you must assign responsibility for your hurt to the proper person. While God may not be *directly* responsible for the injury you've sustained, shouldn't He be charged at the very least with negligence for allowing it to happen?

The good news is that God readily accepts responsibility for *everything* that occurs in His creation. Consider God's words to Moses:

> Who has made man's mouth? Or who makes him dumb or deaf, or seeing or blind? Is it not I, the LORD? (Exodus 4:11)

Some well-meaning Christians, trying to defend God's reputation, prematurely excuse Him from any responsibility for human suffering. "Be assured that God is just as grieved about your baby's deformity as you are. But as much as He wanted to, God could not violate the natural laws of genetics that resulted in your baby's defect." Baloney. God takes full responsibility for all human suffering, including the wrongs others commit against us.

Read carefully Peter's words from his sermon at Pentecost, preached to those who just a few weeks earlier had crucified Christ:

> [T]his Man, delivered up by the predetermined plan and foreknowledge of God, you nailed to a cross by the hands of godless men and put Him to death. (Acts 2:23)

Who was responsible for Christ's death? Godless men nailed him to the cross, but they were only instruments to accomplish God's "predetermined plan."

Now let me ask you a question. If God is willing to accept the blame for creating deformed babies and for the horrific death of His own Son, don't you think His shoulders are broad enough to take responsibility for the hurt *you* have endured?

God's Plan for You Is Conceived in Love

The claim that "God loves you and has a wonderful plan for your life" is more than an effective opener for an evangelistic booklet. The Bible repeatedly affirms that God has planned every detail of our life — every joy as well as every heartache, every success as well as every failure, every triumph as well as every tragedy. All are part of His sovereign plan.

But the Author of that plan is not a capricious deity who arbitrarily moves us around like pawns on a cosmic chessboard. Instead, God's plan for your life — all of it — is based upon His love for you:

> *In Thy lovingkindness* Thou hast led the people whom Thou hast redeemed. (Exodus 15:13)

> Thine eyes have seen my unformed substance;
> And in Thy book they were all written,
> The days that were ordained for me,
> When as yet there was not one of them.
> (Psalm 139:16)

> Man's steps are ordained by the LORD,
> How then can man understand his way?
> (Proverbs 20:24)

> "For I know the plans that I have for you," declares the LORD, "plans for welfare and not for calamity to give you a future and a hope." (Jeremiah 29:11)

God's Plan Is Often Beyond Our Understanding

The previous statements may seem contradictory to you. How could a God who loves you include unjust suffering and indescribable pain in His plan for you?

C. S. Lewis brilliantly exposes the real problem in reconciling God's sovereignty with God's love:

> We want, in fact, not so much a Father in heaven as a grandfather in heaven...whose plan for the universe was simply that it might be truly said at the end of each day, "A good time was had by all."... I should very much like to live in a universe which was governed on such lines. But since it is abundantly clear that I don't, and since I have reason to believe, nevertheless, that God is Love, I conclude that my conception of love needs correction.... The problem of reconciling human suffering with the existence of a God who loves, is only insoluble so long as we attach a trivial meaning to the word "love."[3]

The Bible promises that "God causes all things to work together for good to those who love God, to those who are called according to His purpose" (Romans 8:28). Unfortunately, some people — to echo Lewis — attach a trivial meaning to the word "good." Those who translate that word as "happiness," "prosperity," or "freedom from adversity" are doomed to disappointment. Instead, Paul identifies the "good" that God's plan is designed to accomplish in the next verse:

> For whom He foreknew, He also predestined to become conformed to the image of His Son, that He might be the first-born among many brethren. (8:29)

God has designed a unique plan for your life with *one* purpose in mind: to mold you into the likeness of His Son.

We can see that suffering must have a role in this plan by looking at what is to me one of the most confusing verses in the Bible: "Although He was a Son, He learned obedience from the things which He suffered" (Hebrews 5:8). How is it that Jesus Christ, the perfect Son of God, could "learn" anything — and "obedience" in particular? Wasn't He perfect already? Believe me, this is on my growing list of questions to ask when I land on the shores of heaven.

But one thing I do understand is that God's plan for Christ included intense suffering. Think about it. If God's plan for His own Son included injustice and intense pain, should I be surprised when God's plan for *my* life includes the same?

Occasionally God allows us to see the purpose of our suffering. Let's return to the Joseph story for a moment. Joseph was able to see the hand of God in his experience. Read carefully his speech to his brothers, noticing the numerous references to God's plan:

> And now do not be grieved or angry with yourselves, because you sold me here; *for God* sent me before you to preserve life.... And *God sent me* before you to preserve for you a remnant in the earth.... Now, therefore, it was

> not you who sent me here, *but God.... God* has made me lord of all Egypt.... And as for you, you meant evil against me, *but God* meant it for good in order to bring about this present result, to preserve many people alive. (Genesis 45:5,7-9; 50:20)

Forgiveness becomes much easier when we can look past our offender's motivations and see God's hand supernaturally working all things together for good. But sometimes — in fact *most* times — we have difficulty seeing any good from the pain we suffer.

Consider the story of Job. Here was a man who lost everything: his assets, his children, and finally his health. Job's initial response of faith was followed by a long period of doubt. Job had some serious questions he wanted answered, and for an agonizingly long time God was silent.

Finally, the answer came — but not the answer Job was seeking. Not once did God ever answer the "why" of Job's suffering. Instead, He reminded His creature of His sovereignty:

> Who is this that darkens counsel
> By words without knowledge?
> Now gird up your loins like a man,
> And I will ask you, and you instruct Me!
> Where were you when I laid the foundation of the earth?
> Tell Me, if you have understanding,
> Who set its measurements, since you know?...
> Have you ever in your life commanded the morning,
> And caused the dawn to know its place;
> That it might take hold of the ends of the earth,
> And the wicked be shaken out of it?...

> Will the faultfinder contend with the Almighty?
> Let him who reproves God answer it.
> (Job 38:2-5,12-13; 40:2)

Frederic Buechner summarizes God's monologue this way:

> God doesn't explain. He explodes. He asks Job who he thinks he is anyway. He says that to try to explain the kind of things Job wants explained would be like trying to explain Einstein to a little-neck clam.... God doesn't reveal his grand design. He reveals himself."[4]

God's answer to Job's question about unjust suffering can be answered in two words: "Trust Me."

And God says the same thing to you and me. If, like Joseph, you're able to see how the hurts of others have resulted in something profitable, then you can thank God for His grace. But even when you cannot see God's hand through the fog of your pain, God still asks you to trust Him. He has not forgotten you. He will not forsake you.

Several years ago I listened to a tape of a testimony of the late Christian author Joe Bayly, who knew firsthand about suffering. Joe told about sitting by the bedside of his four-year-old son who was dying from leukemia. His little boy had always had a deep love for Jesus, so it was natural for Joe to want to comfort his son by describing the wonders that awaited him in heaven.

"Daddy, will you and Mommy go with me?"

"No, son, we can't go with you now. We'll come later. But Jesus will be there to meet you and hold you in His arms."

"Then I don't want to go, if you can't go with me."

Joe recalled, "I wish I could say that my son died a peaceful death, full of assurance. But I watched him die a violent death, without the peace I wanted him to have." And Joe and his wife watched two more of their children die in a similar fashion.

Although many people would give up on a God who would allow such a thing to happen, Joe Bayly concluded his earthly life some years ago with his faith firmly intact. When asked about the suffering his family had endured, Joe put it this way: "We can go one of two directions when we can't reconcile a loss with our faith in God. Either we give up that faith in God, or we realize that He's in control and working out a plan, even though in the darkness we cannot see what the plan is. Faith means something when it is exercised in the darkness."

I realize you may well be struggling with the issue of forgiveness. Someone or something has caused great pain in your life. You want to forgive. You're ready to be free from the bitterness that is destroying your life. You've spent hours reading about why and how to forgive. But if you release that person who has wronged you, you need something to grab hold of to maintain your balance in life.

God is saying to you, "Release your bitterness and grab hold of Me. Allow Me to take responsibility for what has happened to you. Know that I have a plan I'm working out in your life, even if you can't see it now. Faith means something when it is exercised in the darkness."

This past week I received a letter from a prisoner who regularly watches our ministry's television broadcast. Usually I can predict with great accuracy the content of such letters: a request for money or a plea for help in obtaining a release. But this letter was different. The prisoner had something he wanted to give me.

He had noticed in my sermon a passing reference to an upcoming series on forgiveness. "About a month ago," he said, "I wrote a poem on forgiveness and thought you might be able to use it in your series." The poem was scrawled on the back of the piece of yellow legal paper.

FORGIVE

by David Aultman

God sent His one and only begotten Son,
To forgive us of all the wrong we have done.
He wants us to do the same thing, too.
He wants you to forgive me and for me to forgive you.
Sometimes it's hard to forget all the wrong,
But we must learn to forgive and to move on.
And if we proceed to live in this way,
God will proceed to forgive us each day.
I must give credit where credit is due,
So Matthew 6:14 tells me this much is true:
One thing to remember for as long as you live,
If you want to be forgiven, then you have to forgive.

David Aultman captured in a few lines what it has taken me two hundred pages to say. The reason we're to forgive is simple: Forgiveness is the obligation of the forgiven.

Another prisoner who lived many years ago said it even more succinctly:

> And be kind to one another, tender-hearted, forgiving
> each other, just as God in Christ also has forgiven you.
> (Ephesians 4:32)

For Further Reflection

A Comprehensive Bible Study on Forgiveness

Chapter 1: The View from the Pulpit
Why the forgiven are not always the best forgivers

1. Imagine that you were in Jerry Fuller's situation (the man who discovered his wife was having an affair). Could you forgive your mate even if he or she were intent on continuing the affair? Why or why not?
2. Is there something in your past for which you have difficulty forgiving yourself? What seems to be the greatest barrier that keeps you from doing so?
3. Do you share Chet Hodgin's belief that it's unfair to ask a victim to forgive an unrepentant offender? Why or why not?
4. In your own words, define "forgiveness."
5. Why do you think people have such a difficult time forgiving others?
6. Explain to what extent you agree with the author's statement that "only the forgiven can truly forgive"?
7. (a) Can you identify one person you are having difficulty forgiving?

(b) Is there something in your life for which you are having difficulty accepting God's forgiveness?

(c) Do you believe, as the author does, that there's probably a connection between your answers to the two preceding questions?

8. What is your initial response to the concept of blaming God for the hurt in our life? Should God be held accountable for our pain? Why or why not?
9. What benefit do you hope to gain from this study on forgiveness?

Chapter 2: The Basis for All Forgiveness

When forgiveness doesn't make sense

1. Have you had a similar experience to that of Dawn Smith Jordan's in which you were confronted with forgiving someone for an inexcusable act? If so, what did you do?
2. In the incident with Jesus described in Luke 7, how were Simon the Pharisee and the prostitute alike? How were they different?
3. Why do self-righteous people have difficulty forgiving others?
4. Why is it sometimes necessary for victims of wrongdoing to take the first step in reconciliation? Does that seem fair to you? Why or why not?
5. What does the story of Adam and Eve teach us about reconciliation? Is there someone in your life with whom you need to take the first step in reconciliation?
6. In your own words, define "grace." Using that definition, can you cite one instance in which you were the recipient of grace from another person? Can you think of a time when you extended grace to another person? How did each experience make you feel?
7. Explain to what extent you agree with this statement: *Grace means overlooking what someone has done to us, just as God has overlooked our sin.*

8. Do you think that a non-Christian can forgive as effectively as a Christian? Why or why not? From your own experience, do you think Christians are skilled in the art of forgiving? Explain.

Chapter 3: Forgiveness on Trial
Three strong arguments against forgiving others

1. Had you been in Simon Wiesenthal's place, would you have forgiven the dying Nazi? Why or why not?
2. What is the difference between forgiving someone's offense and simply overlooking that offense?
3. How can you distinguish between those offenses that should be overlooked and those that need to be forgiven?
4. Which argument *against* forgiving was most convincing to you? Why?
5. Which argument *against* forgiveness is least convincing to you? Why?
6. Which of the four arguments *for* forgiveness is most compelling to you?
7. Is forgiveness an obligation or a choice? Defend your answer.
8. What principles about forgiveness do we learn from Jesus' parable of the two slaves in Matthew 18?

Chapter 4: Forgiveness and Repentance
Why the words "I'm sorry" are highly overrated

1. "Only a person who demonstrates some remorse for his offense should be forgiven." Before reading this chapter, did you agree or disagree with that statement? Has your opinion changed since reading this chapter? If so, in what way?

2. Of the author's three arguments for demanding repentance before offering forgiveness, which seemed strongest to you? Why?
3. In Jesus' story of the prodigal son, when do you think the father actually forgave his rebellious son?
4. What is the problem with demanding that our offender "earn" our forgiveness?
5. If God requires our repentance before forgiving us, why shouldn't we demand the same from our offender?
6. What makes unconditional forgiveness practical?
7. Why is unconditional forgiveness more beneficial than conditional forgiveness?
8. What is the most helpful insight about forgiveness you have gleaned from this chapter?

Chapter 5: Forgiveness and Consequences

Why forgiven people sometimes must sit in the electric chair

1. Have you ever had difficulty distinguishing between forgiveness and consequences? Explain.
2. In your own words, explain the difference between vengeance and justice.
3. Why do you think God prohibits us from seeking vengeance?
4. Imagine that a young woman said to you, "Several years ago I became a Christian and started living a moral lifestyle. However, last week I discovered that I have AIDS. If God has truly forgiven me for my past, why do I have to suffer for sins I turned away from years ago?" How would you answer her?
5. If the leaders in your church discovered that an elder was having an

affair, should that fact be made public to the congregation? If so, under what circumstances?

6. Can you cite an example in your own life in which the negative consequences of a past sin have kept you close to the Lord?
7. Why is it better to allow other people to seek justice for offenses we suffer?
8. Visualize someone who has wronged you and should suffer some consequences for what he has done. Are you willing to release that person to God so that He might avenge the offense?

Chapter 6: Forgiveness and Reconciliation

"I forgive you, but I don't want to have dinner with you (or breakfast or lunch for that matter)"

1. Read through the three counseling situations described at the beginning of this chapter. What advice would you had given *before* reading the rest of the chapter? Would your advice have changed after reading this chapter? If so, in what way?
2. In your own words, explain the difference between forgiveness and reconciliation.
3. Why does a Christian need to confess his sins if God has already forgiven him?
4. Visualize someone who has hurt you in the past. Do you desire to resume your relationship with that person? If not, can you explain why?
5. The author mentions three ingredients necessary for reconciliation. Which of these do you think is most important and why?
6. Is there a way to test the sincerity of someone's repentance? Explain your answer.

7. How would you respond to someone who said, "Since God forgives us unconditionally, we also should try and rebuild broken relationships with anyone who has offended us, even if that person doesn't repent or change"?
8. What one insight from this chapter is particularly applicable to your life right now? Why?

Chapter 7: Forgiveness and Forgetting
Why forgetting pain is neither possible nor profitable

1. Have you ever tried Eisenhower's method of "forgiveness"? Did it work? Why or why not? Are there any situations when it can work?
2. The author mentions two dangers of confusing forgiveness with forgetting. Have you experienced either one of these results? Explain.
3. In your own words, explain the concept of God's forgetting our sins.
4. Why is forgetting another person's offense toward us impossible? Do you think that this inability to forget is a part of God's design, or is it the result of our fallen nature? Explain your answer.
5. Is there a sin in your life you have difficulty forgetting? What positive benefits have you experienced by remembering your failures?
6. How can you distinguish between offenses that can be easily dismissed and those that need to be deliberately forgiven?
7. The author suggests several ways to deal with memories of wrongs we have suffered. Which suggestion do you think is most vital and why?
8. Identify either the sin you've committed that you have most difficulty forgetting or the wrong you've suffered that you have most difficulty forgetting. What one suggestion from this chapter

are you willing to apply this week to help you deal with that memory?

Chapter 8: Receiving the Gift

You can't give away what you don't possess

1. How would you explain the difference between "false guilt" and "legitimate guilt"? Have you ever had difficulty distinguishing between the two?
2. What lessons can we learn about temptation from the story of David's downfall?
3. Have you ever confused God's mercy with His tolerance? Explain.
4. Has reading this chapter brought to your mind any sin for which you need God's forgiveness? Follow the principles outlined in this chapter to experience His cleansing.
5. In a situation such as adultery, should you confess your sin to your spouse if he or she is unaware of that offense? Why or why not?
6. What is the difference between offering an apology and asking for forgiveness?
7. Have you ever had someone refuse to forgive you? What do you think was the reason for that refusal?
8. Ask God to reveal to you someone you have wronged. Will you commit to following the steps outlined in this chapter to seek reconciliation? Write down a simple plan of action you can follow.

Chapter 9: Granting the Gift

The three-step process for letting go of poisonous people in your life

1. Be honest for a moment. Identify several people you would like to "bite."

2. Why is learning how to blame people critical to learning how to forgive? How can you prevent blame from turning into bitterness?
3. The author says that we should not only identify the wrong that has been committed but also calculate the debt owed. Who benefits most from such a calculation — the offender or the offended? Explain your answer.
4. How important is it to be able to identify a specific time when you have forgiven another person? How important is it to be able to specify the exact time you received God's forgiveness?
5. What is the crucial difference between granting forgiveness and receiving forgiveness? Under what circumstances should a person wait to verbalize his forgiveness to his offender?
6. As you look over the names on your list from question 1, which people do you think would be receptive to your forgiveness? Which ones aren't? What reasons do you see for their openness or lack of openness to your forgiveness?
7. Explain to what extent you agree with this statement: *Just as salvation is a one-time act of God, forgiving another person is also a one-time choice we make.*
8. As you've read this chapter, has God brought to your mind the name of someone you need to forgive? If so, look at the suggested prayer under the heading, "True Forgiveness Continually Releases Our Offender of His or Her Obligation." Are you willing to pray that prayer?

Chapter 10: Forgiving God?

Why blaming God for your problems makes more sense than you think

1. Why are other people the easiest targets for our blame?
2. Do you tend to blame yourself for problems in your life? Is it possible for a person to forgive himself? Why or why not?
3. Do you believe that circumstances can be a legitimate source of blame for our problems? Why or why not? If so, can you support your belief from Scripture?
4. Why do you think Satan is so often blamed for evil? Can you identify some mishap in your life for which you hold Satan responsible?
5. Why do you think some people are reluctant to hold God accountable for their suffering?
6. The author discusses the concept of forgiving God. Do you believe forgiving God is ever warranted? Why or why not?
7. Can you recall a hurt you experienced that later turned out for good? Is there some offense you have suffered for which you are still having to trust in God's sovereignty?
8. What is the most beneficial insight you've gained from this book on forgiveness? Complete this sentence: "As a result of this book, I am going to…"

AMERICANS' VIEWS ON FORGIVENESS

A National Opinion Study

The following information is adapted from the reported findings of an opinion study commissioned by WaterBrook Press and conducted by Barna Research Group, Ltd., in July and August 1999. The research was conducted in OmniPoll™. In a nationwide sample 1,002 U.S. adults were asked seven questions focused on their perceptions of forgiveness.

STUDY OBJECTIVES

The researchers had the following objectives:

- To determine the percentage of adults who would admit that they currently had someone in their life whom they had a very difficult time forgiving.
- To determine Americans' views of whether God is responsible for allowing pain and hurt in people's lives.
- To determine the specific beliefs of Americans about what forgiveness is and is not, including:
  1. Should forgiveness be granted only if the offending individual shows remorse?

2. Does true forgiveness require that the offending party be released from the consequences of his or her actions?
3. Does true forgiveness require that the forgiver re-establish a relationship with the offending person?
4. Does true forgiveness mean that the forgiver must also forget what was done?
5. Are there some crimes, offenses, or other things that people do to one another that can never be forgiven?

The contention of the research sponsors is that a biblically informed answer to each of these five questions would be "no." In other words, each of these five questions, when stated in the affirmative, represents what might be termed "myths" about forgiveness:

- *Myth 1:* Forgiveness should be granted only if the offending individual shows remorse.
- *Myth 2:* True forgiveness requires that the offending party be released from the consequences of his or her actions.
- *Myth 3:* True forgiveness requires that the forgiver re-establish a relationship with the offending person.
- *Myth 4:* True forgiveness means that the forgiver must also forget what was done.
- *Myth 5:* There are some crimes, offenses, or other things that people do to one another that can never be forgiven.

The research, then, was designed to explore the percentage of Americans who hold what we have termed a "biblical" view of forgiveness on each of those five elements.

SURVEY METHODOLOGY

The OmniPoll™ included 1,002 telephone interviews conducted among a representative sample of adults over the age of 18 within the

48 contiguous states. The survey was completed in August 1999. All interviews were conducted from the Barna Research Group telephone center in Ventura, California. The sampling error for OmniPoll™ is plus or minus three percentage points, at the 95% confidence level. The survey calls were made at various times during the day and evening.

The average interview lasted twenty minutes. All of the interviews were conducted by experienced, trained interviewers; interviewers were supervised at all times, and every interviewer was monitored, using the Silent Monitoring™ system employed by Barna Research Group. The survey was conducted through the use of the Computer Assisted Telephone Interviewing system, a process that ensures that questioning patterns are properly administered by interviewers and that survey results are recorded accurately.

Based upon U.S. Census data sources, regional and ethnic quotas were designed to ensure that the final group of adults interviewed reflected the distribution of adults nationwide. The final survey data were balanced according to gender.

In this study, the cooperation rate was 84%. This is an unusually high rate (the industry norm is about 60%), and it significantly raises the confidence we may place in the resulting statistics. In every survey there are a variety of ways in which the accuracy of the data may be affected, and the cooperation rate is one such potential cause of error in measurement: the lower the rate, the less representative the respondents may be of the population from which they were drawn, thereby reducing the accuracy of the results. (Other sources of error include question-design bias, question-order bias, interviewer mistakes, sampling error, and respondent deception; many of these types of errors cannot be accurately estimated, but having a high cooperation rate does enhance the reliability of the information procured.)

The survey respondents were classified according to a number of "subgroups," including the following:

Gender — male or female

Age — in the ranges 18 to 33 years ("Busters"), 34 to 52 years ("Boomers"), 53 to 71 years ("Builders"), and 72 years and older (seniors)

Marital status — currently married, currently unmarried, and currently divorced or at one time divorced

Education level — high school or less, some college, or college graduate from a four-year institution

Household annual pretax income — less than $40,000, from $40,000 to $74,000, or $75,000 or more

Political ideology — conservative, moderate, or liberal

Registered to vote — registered at current address or not registered at current address

Region — Northeast, South, Midwest, or West

Ethnicity — white (non-Hispanic), black, Hispanic, or nonwhite (including black, Hispanic, Asian, Native American, and other ethnic groups)

"Born-again": This classification does *not* refer to people calling themselves by this label. The Barna Research Group surveys include two questions regarding beliefs that are used to classify people as born-again or not born-again. To be classified as born-again Christians, individuals must say that they have made a personal commitment to Jesus Christ that is still important in their life today and that after they die, they will go to heaven because they have confessed their sins and accepted Jesus Christ as their Savior. People who meet these criteria are classified as born-again regardless of whether they would describe themselves in that way.

"Evangelical": This term is applied to born-again Christians (as just defined) who also meet seven additional criteria: (1) saying their faith is very important in their life; (2) believing they have a responsibility to

share their faith in Christ with non-Christians; (3) believing in the existence of Satan; (4) believing that eternal salvation is gained through God's grace alone, not through our efforts; (5) believing that Jesus Christ lived a sinless life while on earth; (6) believing the Bible is accurate in all that it teaches; (7) choosing an orthodox definition of God. As defined in this survey report, the term "evangelical" has no relationship to church attendance, church membership, or denominational affiliation.

Denomination: Five major groupings were used: Catholic (those attending a Catholic church); Baptist (those attending a church in one of the Baptist denominations); Methodist (those attending a church in one of the Methodist denominations); mainline (those attending a church within the Episcopal, Methodist, Lutheran, Presbyterian, or United Church of Christ denominations); and Protestant non-mainline (those attending a Protestant denomination other than the five listed in the mainline category).

Self-descriptions: These included "charismatic" (or "Pentecostal"); "theologically conservative"; "theologically liberal"; "church attender"; "not financially comfortable"; and "stressed out."

On the following pages is a summary analysis for each of the seven questions commissioned by WaterBrook Press in this opinion study. Each analysis includes the basic data in response to the survey question, plus important findings and statistically significant patterns in the ways different subgroups answered the question.

Unforgiveness Among U.S. Adults

QUESTION

"There is someone in your life who has hurt you in a way that you find very difficult to forgive." Do you agree or disagree with that statement? Do you (agree/disagree) strongly or somewhat?

RESPONSE

Agree strongly: 27%

Agree somewhat: 11%

Disagree somewhat: 16%

Disagree strongly: 45%

Not sure: 2%

ANALYSIS

Overall, the researchers discovered that nearly four out of ten U.S. adults (38%) agreed with the statement "There is someone in your life who has hurt you in a way that you find very difficult to forgive." About one out of four individuals (27%) strongly agreed with that description of their situation.

From a macro-perspective, that projects to between 55 million and 60 million adults who are struggling to a large extent with the issue of forgiveness in their lives — more specifically, they are struggling because they have been *unable* to forgive someone.

To better interpret the data it may be helpful to analyze the construction of the survey question itself. The survey item was designed to provide a reliable and accurate estimate of the proportion of adults who *currently experience significant difficulty in forgiving someone.* That is different from simply asking people if they have *ever had any difficulty* forgiving someone. Further, the statement asks respondents to classify their experience as one in which it is "very difficult" to forgive their offender.

Given the question wording — and also the fact that there is a relatively small proportion of "middle-of-the-road answers" (such as "agree somewhat" or "disagree somewhat"), we can have increased confidence that these results provide a reliable measurement.

SUBGROUP PATTERNS

The population segments that were more likely to admit struggling with forgiveness were intriguing. People who are divorced, those who said they are stressed out, individuals at the lower end of the socio-economic scale, blacks, "Busters," Baptists, nonvoters, and singles were more likely than average to say that they currently experience significant difficulty forgiving someone.

Overall, one out of four born-again Christians (23%) and one out of ten evangelical Christians (10%) said that there is someone they have not been able to forgive.

Below is a numeric profile of the subgroups that were either more likely or less likely to say they struggle to forgive someone.

(*Average:* 27% of U.S. adults strongly agreed that there was someone whom they found very difficult to forgive.)

Segments MOST likely to struggle with forgiveness:

- those with the self-description: stressed out (41%)
- divorced people (37%)
- blacks (36%)
- Baptists (34%)
- singles (34%)
- nonwhites (34%)
- those not registered to vote (34%)
- "Busters" (34%)
- those with the self-description: not financially comfortable (32%)
- those with an annual income under $40,000 (31%)

Segments LEAST likely to struggle with forgiveness:

- evangelical Christians (10%)
- Methodists (14%)

- those with an annual income of $75,000 or more (15%)
- college graduates (17%)
- people who are married (19%)
- mainline Protestant church attenders (20%)
- church attenders (21%)
- adults over 54 ("Builders" and seniors) (21%)
- born-again Christians (23%)
- registered voters (24%)
- whites (24%)

Perception of God's Role in Allowing Pain

QUESTION

"You believe that God is ultimately responsible for allowing pain and hurt in your life." Do you agree or disagree with that statement? Do you (agree/disagree) strongly or somewhat?

RESPONSE

Agree strongly: 14%
Agree somewhat: 10%
Disagree somewhat: 17%
Disagree strongly: 55%
Not sure: 5%

ANALYSIS

A majority of U.S. adults (55%) strongly objected to the notion that God is "ultimately responsible" for allowing pain and hurt in their lives. When including those individuals who said that they disagree somewhat, the researchers discovered that more than seven out of ten adults (72%) did not concur with the statement.

Overall, only about one out of seven adults (14%) believes strongly that God is ultimately responsible for allowing the pain and hurt in their lives.

SUBGROUP PATTERNS

Even among the subgroups most likely to believe that God is responsible for the best and worst in life, only a minority agreed strongly with the statement. These groups include evangelical Christians, seniors, church attenders, born-again Christians, and individuals who attend non-mainline Protestant churches.

Listed below are the subgroups who were either more likely or less likely to say they strongly believe God is ultimately responsible for allowing pain and hurt in their lives.

(*Average:* 14% of U.S. adults strongly agreed with the biblical perspective that God is ultimately responsible for allowing pain and hurt in their lives.)

Segments MOST likely to believe that God has the ultimate responsibility:

- evangelical Christians (29%)
- seniors (28%)
- church attenders (18%)
- born-again Christians (18%)
- non-mainline Protestant church attenders (18%)
- political conservatives (17%)
- theological conservatives (17%)

Segments LEAST likely to believe that God has the ultimate responsibility:

- political liberals (7%)
- those with an annual income above $75,000 (9%)
- "Boomers" (10%)
- non-Christians (11%)

Myth 1: Forgiveness Requires the Offender's Remorse

QUESTION

"You cannot honestly forgive someone unless that person shows some remorse for what they did." Do you think that is a very accurate, somewhat accurate, not too accurate, or not at all accurate description of forgiveness?

RESPONSE

Very accurate: 30%
Somewhat accurate: 32%
Not too accurate: 11%
Not at all accurate: 25%
Not sure: 3%

ANALYSIS

Overall, one out of four U.S. adults (25%) strongly concurred with the biblical principle that you can honestly forgive someone even if that individual does not show remorse for what he or she did. (Another 11% of adults expressed moderate agreement with the principle.)

Conversely, three out of five individuals (62%) believe that the offender must demonstrate some sort of remorse in order to warrant forgiveness.

SUBGROUP PATTERNS

This myth generated some of the most intriguing patterns in terms of how a person's faith affected his or her views. While just one out of five non-Christians (18%) firmly believes that you should forgive someone even if that person has not expressed remorse for the offense, one-third of born-again Christians (33%) embraced this notion. Among evangelical Christians, three out of five (60%) said that forgiveness does not depend upon the remorse of the offender.

The upshot of faith differences? Although born-again Christians are *statistically* more likely to believe differently than non-Christians, in *practical* terms the difference is relatively minor. Only a minority of each group — one out of five non-Christians and one out of three born-again Christians — holds a biblical perspective about forgiveness on this issue.

Evangelical Christians (as defined by their biblical perspective on nine issues) demonstrated a marked difference from other respondents, with nearly two out of three holding a biblical view of forgiveness on this subject.

(*Average:* 25% of U.S. adults strongly agree with the biblical perspective that you can honestly forgive someone even if that person does not show any remorse for his or her actions.)

Segments MOST likely to hold this biblical perspective about forgiveness:

- evangelical Christians (60%)
- college graduates (35%)
- born-again Christians (33%)
- "Boomers" (29%)
- those who are married (28%)

Segments LEAST likely to hold this biblical perspective about forgiveness:

- non-Christians (18%)
- Catholics (19%)
- those not registered to vote (19%)
- nonwhites (20%)

- singles (21%)
- those with the self-description: stressed out (21%)

Myth 2: Forgiveness Requires Release from Consequences

QUESTION

"If you really forgive someone, you would want that person to be released from the consequences of their actions." Do you think that is a very accurate, somewhat accurate, not too accurate, or not at all accurate description of forgiveness?

RESPONSE

Very accurate: 28%
Somewhat accurate: 32%
Not too accurate: 13%
Not at all accurate: 23%
Not sure: 4%

ANALYSIS

Overall, nearly one out of four U.S. adults (23%) strongly believes that you can really forgive someone and still maintain that the offender should be held responsible for the consequences of his or her actions. Altogether, about one-third of the population (36%) believes that forgiveness does *not* equate to overlooking consequences.

Conversely, more than half of U.S. adults (60%) maintain that when you forgive someone you should also want that person to be released from the consequences of his or her actions; 28% said that this perspective was a very accurate description of true forgiveness.

SUBGROUP PATTERNS

Interestingly, this principle seemed to correlate strongly with socio-economic status and education levels. Affluent, well-educated adults were more likely than less affluent, less educated respondents to believe that forgiveness does *not* require that consequences be overlooked. "Boomers," registered voters, and whites — groups accustomed to a high degree of control over their environment and circumstances — were more likely than average to contend that forgiveness can occur even while hoping that the offender receives the just consequences of his or her actions.

Whether or not a person was a Christian — born-again or evangelical — was not correlated with having a biblical perspective on this issue.

(*Average:* 23% of U.S. adults strongly agree with the biblical perspective that true forgiveness can occur even without wanting the offender to be released from the consequences of his or her actions.)

Segments MOST likely to hold this biblical perspective about forgiveness:

- those with an annual income over $75,000 (35%)
- college graduates (33%)
- "Boomers" (27%)
- registered voters (25%)
- whites (25%)

Segments least likely to hold this biblical perspective about forgiveness:

- Hispanics (12%)
- those with the self-description: charismatic/Pentecostal (16%)
- nonwhites (18%)
- those with an annual income below $40,000 (18%)
- those not registered to vote (18%)

- people with an education of high school or less (19%)
- non-mainline Protestant church attenders (20%)
- theological conservatives (20%)

Myth 3: Forgiveness Requires Rebuilding the Relationship

QUESTION

"If you genuinely forgive someone, you should rebuild your relationship with that person." Do you think that is a very accurate, somewhat accurate, not too accurate, or not at all accurate description of forgiveness?

RESPONSE

Very accurate: 35%
Somewhat accurate: 38%
Not too accurate: 12%
Not at all accurate: 13%
Not sure: 2%

ANALYSIS

On average, nearly three out of four people (73%) believe that genuine forgiveness necessitates the rebuilding of your relationship with the offending person.

Only one out of four adults (25%) contends that when you forgive someone you are not necessarily obligated to rebuild the relationship with that person; only 13% felt strongly about this notion.

SUBGROUP PATTERNS

An average of 13% of U.S. adults strongly agreed with the biblical perspective that true forgiveness can occur even if the forgiver does not rebuild his or her relationship with the offending person. The segments *most* likely to hold this biblical perspective about forgiveness were political liberals (22%) and Midwesterners (17%). No groups were found to be significantly *less* likely than average to hold this biblical perspective.

Myth 4: Forgiveness Means Forgetting What Happened

QUESTION

"If you have really forgiven someone, you should be able to forget what they have done to you." Do you think that is a very accurate, somewhat accurate, not too accurate, or not at all accurate description of forgiveness?

RESPONSE

Very accurate: 32%
Somewhat accurate: 34%
Not too accurate: 12%
Not at all accurate: 22%
Not sure: 1%

ANALYSIS

Overall, two-thirds (66%) of the U.S. population agrees that forgetting must accompany forgiveness.

On the other hand, one-third (33%) of adults nationwide disagreed either moderately or strongly. These individuals contend that if you really forgive someone, you *may or may not* be able to forget what that person did. About one out of five adults (22%) expressed the belief that the statement was not at all an accurate description of forgiveness.

SUBGROUP PATTERNS

College graduates were the only segment that was more likely than average to hold the biblical perspective on forgiving and forgetting. Still, only one-third of college grads (32%) held the biblical perspective.

In terms of religious variables, born-again and evangelical Christians were no different than the average. Interestingly, Baptists and adults who attend non-mainline Protestant churches were actually less likely than average to hold the biblical view on this issue. That finding suggests the possibility that within these denominational circles, forgiving and forgetting are often linked as biblically consistent concepts.

(*Average:* 22% of U.S. adults strongly agreed with the biblical perspective that forgiveness does not necessitate forgetting what happened.)

The segment MOST likely to hold this biblical perspective about forgiveness:

- college graduates (32%)

Segments LEAST likely to hold this biblical perspective about forgiveness:

- Baptists (16%)
- people with an education of high school or less (18%)
- non-mainline Protestant church attenders (18%)
- theological conservatives (18%)

Myth 5: Some Offenses Are Not Forgivable

QUESTION

"There are some crimes, offenses, or other things that people can do to one another that are so bad they should never be forgiven." Do you think that is a very accurate, somewhat accurate, not too accurate, or not at all accurate description of forgiveness?

RESPONSE

Very accurate: 23%

Somewhat accurate: 27%

Not too accurate: 13%

Not at all accurate: 34%

Not sure: 4%

ANALYSIS

About one-third of adults (34%) firmly hold the biblical perspective that there are no crimes or offenses people can commit that are unforgivable. Another 13% of adults moderately agree with this perspective.

In contrast, half of adults (50%) said they believe that some offenses can never be forgiven.

SUBGROUP PATTERNS

Evangelical Christians and born-again Christians were much more likely than average to hold the biblical perspective that none of our offenses against one another should be classified as unforgivable. Still, only half of born-again Christians (50%) held this biblical view. Non-Christians (21%) were the least likely subgroup to hold the biblical perspective about forgiveness when it came to this issue.

(*Average:* 34% of U.S. adults strongly agreed with the biblical perspective that there are no offenses too extreme for us to forgive.)

Segments MOST likely to hold this biblical perspective about forgiveness:

- evangelical Christians (72%)
- born-again Christians (50%)
- "Builders" (45%)
- church attenders (44%)

- non-mainline Protestant church attenders (44%)
- Baptists (42%)
- college graduates (41%)
- Southerners (40%)
- people who are married (37%)
- registered voters (37%)

Segments LEAST likely to hold this biblical perspective about forgiveness:

- non-Christians (21%)
- Catholics (26%)
- those not registered to vote (27%)
- mainline Protestant church attenders (28%)
- Northeasterners (28%)
- theological liberals (29%)
- "Busters" (29%)
- singles (30%)

A Biblical Worldview on Forgiveness

Previous surveys in the Barna Research Group's exploration of faith in America have illustrated that very few born-again Christians possess a biblical worldview — a well-rounded philosophy of life that helps them interpret and react to the world around them in a biblical fashion. It appears that millions of well-meaning, born-again Christians fail to *act* as a Christian should because they do not *think* as a Christian should.

What about forgiveness? Do most adults have a biblical viewpoint about forgiveness? Do most Christians? The conclusion emerging from this research is that probably very few Americans (and only a small handful of born-again Christians) have a coherent, biblical worldview of forgiveness.

For instance, based on the five "myths" about forgiveness which the researchers examined, only 4% of respondents gave the biblical response to all five. Among born-again Christians, only 5% disagreed with all five myths. Among evangelical Christians — an ardent subset of the born-again segment — just 8% held the biblical perspective about forgiveness on all five issues.

BIBLICAL FORGIVERS

We can also look at the data another way. One out of five adults (20%) disagreed strongly with at least three of the five myths; the researchers grouped these respondents into a category of those who essentially held a biblical perspective about forgiveness. (The population segments *most* likely to fit into this grouping of "biblical forgivers" included college graduates, born-again Christians, and evangelicals. The segments *least* likely to have a biblical perspective about forgiveness included "Builders," seniors, non-Christians, those who attend a Protestant mainline church, individuals with a high school education or less, blacks, residents of the South, and people who are divorced.)

The study's findings further suggest that most born-again Christians probably do not practice biblical forgiveness because they do not understand what it is. Overall, only one out of four (25%) individuals classified as born-again Christians fit into the category of those who embrace biblical forgiveness (those who disagreed strongly with at least three of the five myths). Among evangelical Christians, the ratio was two out of five — 40%.

While born-again Christians differed from non-Christians in terms of their likelihood to embrace a biblical perspective about forgiveness, in practical terms the difference is marginal: One out of seven non-Christians (15%) held a biblical perspective about forgiveness, while among born-again Christians the ratio is one out of four (25%). It appears that born-again Christians' perspectives about forgiveness are not distinguishable from non-Christians on any widespread or systematic basis.

Biblical Forgivers and the Five Myths

Among the 20% of U.S. adults who fit in the "biblical perspective" category as previously identified, there were varying levels of agreement with the biblical perspective regarding the five forgiveness "myths." For each of the five myths, here are the percentages of these "biblical perspective" respondents who strongly *disagreed*:

Myth 1 (the offender must feel remorse): 67%.

Myth 2 (the offender must be released from consequences): 61%.

Myth 3 (genuine forgiveness requires rebuilding the relationship with the offender): 41%.

Myth 4 (genuine forgiveness means forgetting what happened): 63%.

Myth 5: (some offenses are not forgivable): 73%

Some intriguing patterns emerge among those holding the biblical perspective. For example, they are most likely to dispute the myth that some offenses are unforgivable. Also, if there is a gap in their understanding about forgiveness, it is that many of these "biblical forgivers" incorrectly believe that the forgiver is required to try rebuilding the damaged relationship with the offender.

Chapter 1

1. Les Alexander, "Nickie Boyd says she believes in forgiveness utterly and completely, but she can't forgive herself," posted 4 April 1996 by the *News & Record* and *Triad Online.*
2. Les Alexander, "Chet Hodgin of Jamestown is adamant about not forgiving the men who killed his two sons," posted 4 April 1996 by the *News & Record* and *Triad Online.*
3. David Seamands, author's file; source unknown.
4. "Americans' Views on Forgiveness," research commissioned by WaterBrook Press and conducted by Barna Research Group, Ltd., Ventura, California, in August 1999; 14.
5. Lewis Smedes, *The Art of Forgiving* (New York: Ballantine, 1996), 178.

Chapter 2

1. Transcript of testimony by Dawn Smith Jordan given at First Baptist Church, Wichita Falls, Texas, on 10 September 1995.
2. Aleksandr I. Solzhenitsyn, *The Gulag Archipelago* (New York: Harper & Row, 1973), 168.
3. Philip Yancey, *What's So Amazing about Grace?* (Grand Rapids, Mich.: Zondervan, 1997), 45.
4. Yancey, *What's So Amazing about Grace?* 67.
5. John F. MacArthur, *The Freedom and Power of Forgiveness* (Wheaton, Ill.: Crossway, 1998), 113-4.

Chapter 3

1. Lewis Smedes, *Forgive & Forget* (New York: HarperCollins, 1996), 126-7.
2. Jane Hindman, as quoted in Robert Jeffress, *Choose Your Attitudes, Change Your Life* (Wheaton, Ill.: Victor, 1992), 100-1.
3. As recounted by Smedes in *The Art of Forgiving*, 37-8.
4. As quoted by Yancey in *What's So Amazing about Grace?* 55.
5. MacArthur, *The Freedom and Power of Forgiveness*, 161.
6. Buechner, Frederick, *Wishful Thinking: A Seeker's ABC* (1973; reprint, revised and expanded, San Francisco: HarperSanFrancisco, 1993), 2.

Chapter 4

1. Tim Jackson, *When Forgiveness Seems Impossible* (Grand Rapids, Mich.: Radio Bible Class, 1994), 11.
2. As quoted by MacArthur in *The Freedom and Power of Forgiveness*, 117-8.
3. As quoted by Charles R. Swindoll in *The Grace Awakening* (Dallas: Word, 1990), 39-40.
4. Max Lucado, *In the Grip of Grace* (Dallas: Word, 1996), 116-7.
5. MacArthur, *The Freedom and Power of Forgiveness,* 122.
6. Jackson, *When Forgiveness Seems Impossible,* 24-5.
7. Chuck Lynch, *I Should Forgive, But…* (Nashville: Word, 1998), 96-9.

Chapter 5

1. Ron Lee Davis, *A Forgiving God in Our Unforgiving World* (Eugene, Oreg.: Harvest House, 1984), 95-6.
2. Smedes, *The Art of Forgiving,* 7-8.
3. Ron Mehl, *The Ten(der) Commandments* (Sisters, Oreg.: Multnomah, 1998), 28.
4. Robert Jeffress, *Say Goodbye to Regret* (Sisters, Oreg.: Multnomah, 1998), 176-7.
5. Charles R. Swindoll, *David* (Dallas: Word, 1997), 210.

Chapter 6

1. As quoted by Charles R. Swindoll in *Laugh Again* (Dallas: Word, 1991), 175.
2. As quoted by Swindoll, *Laugh Again,* 83.
3. Smedes, *The Art of Forgiving,* 27.

Chapter 7

1. As quoted by Gary Inrig in *The Parables* (Grand Rapids, Mich.: Discovery House, 1991), 68.
2. Lynch, *I Should Forgive*, 27.
3. David W. Augsburger, *Seventy Times Seven* (Chicago: Moody, 1970), 19.
4. Lynch, *I Should Forgive,* 36.
5. As quoted in Jeffress, *Say Goodbye to Regret,* 141.

Chapter 8

1. Bill Gothard, Institute in Basic Youth Conflicts Syllabus, 1969, Oak Brook, Illinois.
2. Gothard, Conflicts Syllabus.

Chapter 9

1. Inrig, *The Parables,* 63.
2. *Parade* magazine, 23 April 1995, 5.
3. Smedes, *The Art of Forgiving,* 178.

Chapter 10

1. Mehl, *The Ten(der) Commandments,* 49-50.
2. Smedes, *Forgive & Forget,* 82.
3. C. S. Lewis, *The Problem of Pain* (New York: Macmillan, 1944), 28, 36.
4. As quoted by Yancey in *Disappointment with God* (Grand Rapids, Mich.: Zondervan, 1988), 190.

Printed in the United States
by Baker & Taylor Publisher Services